CREATIVE
SOCIALS
AND
SPECIAL
EVENTS

Other Zondervan/Youth Specialties Books

CREATIVE
SOCIALS
AND
SPECIAL
EVENTS

WAYNE RICE AND MIKE YACONELLI

ZONDERVAN PUBLISHING HOUSE
Grand Rapids, Michigan

CREATIVE SOCIALS AND SPECIAL EVENTS
Copyright © 1986 by Youth Specialties, Inc.

Youth Specialties Books are published
by the Zondervan Publishing House
1415 Lake Drive, S.E.
Grand Rapids, Michigan 49506

Library of Congress Cataloging in Publication Data

Rice, Wayne.
  Creative socials and special events.

  1. Church work with youth—Handbooks, manuals, etc. 2. Church group work with youth—
Handbooks, manuals, etc. I. Yaconelli, Mike. II. Title.
BV4447.R46 1986   259'.2   86-15831
ISBN 0-310-35131-6

Edited by David Lambert
Designed by Ann Cherryman
Illustrated by Corbin Hillam

Printed in the United States of America

89 90 91 92 93 94 95 / AK / 14 13 12 11 10 9 8 7 6

Contents

Introduction

Welcome to the Youth Ministry Toy Department. Along this aisle labeled "How-to-Make-Youth-Work-Fun" are dozens of the world's best and most creative social activities—party and fellowship ideas that are perfect for a weekend night, a Saturday or Sunday afternoon, or any holiday of the year. Browsing through the department, you'll find ideas you can use anytime, anywhere, and for almost any occasion.

The special events and social activities here will serve lots of purposes; perhaps the most obvious is simply *to have fun*. Today's kids, as different as they are from the kids of a generation ago, are no different in one way: They like to have fun. They have a great need to play, to laugh, and to interact with each other in a casual, nonthreatening environment.

Good special events for teens should be fun without being juvenile. Young people need opportunities to have a good time without getting into trouble or getting stoned—a new experience for some kids. Many of today's young people seem to have lost the ability to play. That's why this book is so important because it will help you provide some good, fun experiences for kids in your youth group—experiences they will never forget.

Another important purpose of special events is *fellowship*, helping kids to get to know each other better and helping the group to build community. When people are interacting positively, communicating with each other, playing together, laughing together, they are being drawn into closer, more trusting relationships with each other.

Special events are also excellent *outreach* activities, which become an important point of contact with new kids. They provide a safe place for your kids to invite their friends, thereby introducing them to the youth group or the youth program of the church. It's often hard for a young person to invite a friend to a Bible study or to a church service, but it's not hard to invite someone to a POLAROID SCAVENGER HUNT or a FAST FOOD PROGRESSIVE DINNER.

Still, be careful. Although special events can and should be used for outreach, don't use them to trap new kids—don't lock the doors and pass out the Bibles. Just use the event as an opportunity to meet new kids, to get to know them, and to make them feel comfortable being a part of your group. Then, they'll be more likely to return or attend other activities.

A balanced youth program will almost always include special events and socials on a regular basis. Some youth groups have a special event once a week; others only once every three or four months; most at least once a month. The frequency of special events and socials for your group depends on you and the needs of your group.

When you are choosing ideas from this book and planning special events for your group, remember that variety is important. Don't do the *same* or the *same kind* of event again and again. There are lots of ideas from which to choose, and most of them can be changed, adapted, or combined with others to create a brand-new special event of your own. Of course, some activities may be so well liked, you'll want to make them an annual tradition; however, it's usually best to keep trying new ones.

Most of the ideas in this book are useable with any size youth group, but some are more fun and effective with a larger group. If your youth group is small, consider planning some of these with another youth group, which might make the event even more special and more exciting for your kids.

Plan your events far enough ahead to get them on everyone's

calendar and promote them well. It's hard for many youth workers to find a date when the kids or their families don't have something else planned. Avoid that problem by making sure the parents, as well as the kids, know about the event as early as possible.

Good promotion for special events and socials is extremely important. While most of the special events in this book will sell themselves, you'll want to generate as much interest and enthusiasm for the event as possible. Here are some ways to advertise your next special event.

1. Use the *mail*. Send out a special flyer, announcement, or invitation, which provides all the details. Make sure the mailer is attractive, up-to-date, and communicates well. If you are having a wild and crazy event, then your announcement should also be a little wild and crazy.

2. Use *creative announcements* in your youth-group meetings. Incorporate announcements into skits, charades, and songs, then present them at unexpected times. For example, if you've planned a beach event, have someone toss a giant beach ball into your meeting with the details of the event painted on its side or have someone walk into the meeting unannounced wearing a bathing suit and sunglasses with the details printed on his beach towel. Use your imagination.

3. Hang *posters* around the church or the youth-group's meeting room several weeks in advance. Again, the more creative and unusual, the better. Perhaps you'll want to use an overhead projector as a poster projector. Make your poster on an overhead transparency, then shine it on the wall or screen.

4. Set up a *telephone chain*. A few days before the event, contact everyone in the youth group by telephone. A personal invitation is hard to turn down.

5. Set up a *youth-group hot line*, a telephone line with an automatic answering machine that provides information about upcoming events.

6. Print some *handouts* that are small and easy for kids to take to school and distribute to their friends. They'll work best if they are funny and clever. Details of the event can be included, or the handout can just announce, "For a great time, call [number of hot line described above]."

Make sure that someone takes pictures at all your special events. The kids will want to come back the following week (or whenever) to see all the pictures. Just before a coming event, display them on the bulletin board or show them in a youth meeting. When the kids see and remember how much fun they had last time, they'll look forward to what's coming.

For *all* special events, planning is of the utmost importance. These guidelines may be useful.

1. Keep in mind the *purpose* of the event and plan accordingly. Know why you are doing what you are doing. If the purpose of the event is primarily outreach, for example, then plan something that will appeal to unchurched kids.

2. Keep in mind the *needs* of the group. The age, sex, social make-up, and physical limitations of the kids will affect your plans.

3. Choose your *location* wisely. Make sure it will accommodate the activities, decorations, and the size of the group. If it is out-of-doors, consider the weather.

4. Choose events where *everyone can participate*, regardless of skill or ability. Emphasize the fun, rather than the competitive, aspect of the activity. Make sure everyone is having such a good time that winning or losing the games becomes irrelevant.

5. Take *safety* precautions. Whether you are using cars, busses, or other transportation, make sure you have drivers who are qualified and vehicles that are in good working condition. If games or activities are rough or have the potential for injury, take care to minimize risk.

6. Be *prepared*. Always have more games or entertainment planned than you need. It is better to be overprepared than to find yourself sitting around with time on your hands and nothing to do. Be *sensitive* to the group as well. If a game or activity at the special event is not popular, switch to another. Begin on time, end on time, and stop when the event is at its peak. Don't let special events fizzle out.

7. Do not *force* participation, encourage it.

8. Do not *embarrass* anyone if you can avoid it.

9. Keep things in *good taste.* Try not to offend anyone needlessly.

10. Make sure you have adequate *adult supervision* and encourage the adults to participate with the kids, rather than simply acting as policemen. Help adults to enjoy themselves as they do the activity with the kids.

11. *Set up ahead of time.* Don't wait until the last minute to decorate or set up for games. Allow plenty of time for emergencies and last-minute changes.

12. Have something for the *early arrivers* to do.

13. Provide *refreshments.* Don't overlook this very important ingredient in youth ministry.

14. Keep a *positive* attitude during the event. Greet everyone in a friendly and enthusiastic manner when they arrive and set a tone of good, lighthearted fun, which will be contagious. Your attitude will give the kids, as well as the adults, permission to relax and enjoy themselves.

Many of the ideas here can be planned and led by members of the youth group; others are better when planned and led by the adult leaders. Be sensitive to this. While the kids' involvement is almost always a good goal, there are times when it is best for the leaders to provide an activity for the kids, so all they have to do is come. Sometimes this element of surprise makes an event successful.

We think you'll discover that the special events in this book will work well with your youth group, since they have already worked well with somebody else's youth group. Almost all of the ideas in this book appeared originally in the *Ideas* library, published by Youth Specialties. They were designed and contributed by a special group of creative youth workers who used them with their own youth groups. Without them, this book would have been impossible. Our sincere thanks to each one of them for their willingness to share their good ideas with us and with you.

★ CHAPTER ONE ★
Theme Events

All of the special events in this chapter are events that are built around a particular unifying theme. This is perhaps the most common kind of special event. For decades, people have enjoyed popular theme events, such as the Sweethearts Banquet, the Grad Night Party, or the Sadie Hawkins Day. Holidays, too, have provided good themes for socials and parties over the years, such as Christmas, Spook Nights, and Fourth-of-July Picnics.

In most cases, events of this type feature games, refreshments, decorations, costumes, and other activities—all centered around the chosen theme. If the event were an Old Timey Night, for example, then everyone might wear Old Timey clothes, play Old Timey games, hear some Old Timey music, and eat some Old Timey food.

Theme events can be used very successfully with youth groups if the theme captures the imagination and sparks the interest of the kids, so pick themes that are exciting enough, crazy enough, or dumb enough to sound exciting and be fun. Plan a Nerd Night, a Banana Night, or a Guinness-Book-of-World-Records Night. Many kids would probably much rather come to a Noise Night than a traditional Valentine's Party.

Although this chapter offers dozens of successful ideas for theme events, remember that the best theme events are those that you create yourself. Here's how.

Pick a theme—almost any will work. You might ask the kids to think of a theme or get ideas from television (note the FANTASY ISLAND NIGHT in this chapter), the movies, popular music, or current fads. Then, brainstorm ideas for games, activities, events, and refreshments. You'll be amazed at the results. Besides, being creative can be a lot of fun, too. Here are some theme events to help you begin.

★ APATHY PARTY

The theme of this event is (ho-hum) *boredom.* Carried to its extremes, it can be a million laughs and anything but boring. Advertise it in the most *boring* ways possible, which actually will attract a lot of attention. Ask the kids to dress as if they just didn't care—to wear the blandest and most boring clothes.

When the kids arrive, have the sponsors greet them at the door and hand out a list of rules for the party, like the ones below. Give the sponsors a few paper bags large enough to put over the heads of anyone who laughs, gets excited, or shows any enthusiasm whatsoever.

Apathy Party Rules

Not Allowed:
Laughing (giggling, chuckling)
Crying
Smiling (grinning)
Frowning (scowling)
Loud voices (neither happy nor angry)
Fast movements
Bright eyes
Enthusiastic hand gestures
Applause
Interesting conversations
Exclamations (wow, oh boy)

Allowed:
Yawning

Bored looks (glazed eyes, rolling eyes)
Slow movements
Tapping fingers
Twiddling thumbs
Monotone voice
Boring conversations
Staring into space
Sleep

Note: If you are caught breaking the rules, you must put a sack over your head until you are able to control yourself and behave in a properly bored manner. Have a real ho-hum time.

The following games can be played at this party.

1. *Undramatic Reading:* Have some books of prose and poetry, perhaps a phone book or dictionary available for finding selections. Ask each person to read a selection from the material as unemotionally and dully as possible. Judges determine the winner.

2. *Clothes Judging:* Have everyone line up and the sponsors judge everyone's clothing. The winner will be the one with the blahest clothes.

3. *Deadpan Face Staring Contest:* Everyone is paired off, and at the signal, kids try to outstare their partner. The winner is the one who stares the longest without laughing, looking away, or closing his eyes. Blinking is permitted. Each contestant may say things to get the other one to laugh but must not get excited himself.

4. *Balancing-Air-on-a-Spoon Relay:* Announce that you were going to have them play a relay where they were to balance a raw egg on a spoon, but you just weren't in the mood to go to the store. So, they must balance air instead. Play the relay normally, but the sponsors determine who has dropped the air off his spoon and ask him go back and start over again. The first team to finish is disqualified for trying too hard. The last-place team is disqualified for trying to lose.

Other games can be played in a similar fashion, or you can announce that all the rest of the games were canceled due to lack of interest. Conclude with some boring slides, boring movies, or some boring skits, presenting awards for the most boring activities or people of the year in your youth group. Serve some lukewarm, half-baked refreshments—for example, defizzed soda pop and melted ice cream. It may taste boring, but your kids will love it.

★ BACKWARD NIGHT

As the name implies, everything about this special event is *done in reverse*. Invitations and posters should be printed backward (even from bottom to top), and oral announcements should be made with your back to the crowd.

As the kids arrive, they should use the back door of the building. Signs leading the way should be spelled backward. Everyone should come to this event with their clothes on backward and inside out.

When the kids arrive, greet them, "Good-by, we hope you had a great time!" Continue the program exactly in reverse, so begin with a devotional if you usually end with one. As the kids leave, put name tags on them, welcome them, and introduce visitors. If paper plates are used for refreshments, use them upside down and make everyone eat wrong-handed.

Divide the group into four or more teams for the following games. Each team begins with one thousand points, then they lose points as they win. The team names can be barnyard animals, and the BARN-YARD game played—each team member makes the sound of his team's animal in the dark and tries to find the rest of his team. On Backward Night, the sounds are reversed, such as ooooom (cow), wow-bow (dog), haw-hee (donkey).

Here are a few other good games for a Backward Night.

1. *Backward Charades:* This game is like regular charades, but the titles must be acted out in reverse. For example, *Gone with the Wind* would be *Wind the with Gone*.

2. *Backward Letter Scramble:* Prepare ahead of time four sets of cards (one set per team) with the letters B-A-C-K-W-A-R-D on them. The cards are passed out to the teams, and each team member holds one or more cards, depending on how many kids are on each team. The leader calls out a word using those letters (examples: drab, raw, bark, crab). The kids holding those letters must line up with their letters, spelling the named word *backward*. First team to do so wins.

3. *Relay Games:* Use any relay game you like, but run it *backward*— kids run backward, crawl backward, and walk backward.

4. *Behind-the-Back Pass:* Teams line up shoulder-to-shoulder. Several objects are then passed down the line from player to player behind their backs. The first team to pass a certain number of these objects to the end of the line is the winner. For fun, try using cups of water. Spilling is a penalty, and points will be added to the score.

★ **BANANA NIGHT**

The Banana Night has, over the years, become one of the most popular of all the creative theme events for youth groups. It has been done in hundreds of youth groups all across America, and some youth groups have gone so far as to make their Banana Night an annual event. It started out as a simple idea—an evening of activities centered around the lowly banana—but as the event has evolved, it has spawned dozens of crazy games and activities, all with a banana theme. Some of those are listed below.

To advertise your Banana Night, put up signs and posters inviting kids to "Go Bananas at Banana Night." They should wear banana colors—yellow, green, or brown (overripe). Their ticket to the event can be one ripe banana to be ripped in half like a normal ticket at the door. As kids arrive, give them banana stickers (available from your local produce distributor) to place on their bodies for the major brands of bananas. The room should be appropriately decorated in early American Banana.

After the kids arrive, divide into bunches (teams) and play any of the following games.

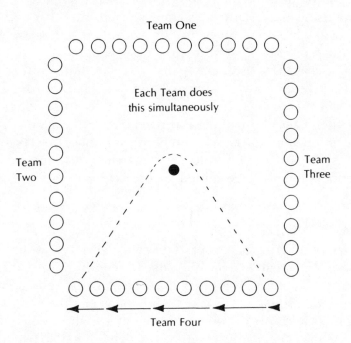

1. *Banana Relay:* Teams line up in a square and sit in chairs or on the floor. Each team is on one side of the square. A chair or some other marker is placed in the middle of the square. A nice, ripe banana is given to each team. At a signal, the first person takes the banana, runs around the center chair, then takes the vacant seat at the opposite end of his team line, while the rest of the team scoots down one seat. Then, the banana is passed down the line from person to person until it reaches the first person in line, and the game continues. When the original first person again has the banana, he must eat the banana to win.

2. *Bobbing for Bananas:* They float, so you can bob for bananas.

3. *Shoot-Out at the O.K. Banana:* Have contestants stick a banana in their holsters (pockets) and quickdraw them like a gunfight. When they draw their bananas, they peel them and eat them. The first shooter with an empty mouth is the winner.

4. *The Un-Banana Race:* Each team chooses one person to eat a banana and drink a bottle (or can) of 7-UP in the fastest time. This normally results in the contestants foaming at the mouth, especially if the 7-UP is warm.

5. *Pass the Banana:* Each team sits in a circle with their feet toward the center. At the signal, a banana is passed from one person to another via feet. If the banana is dropped, the person who dropped it becomes the beginning of a new circle, and the banana must be passed completely around again. Each team is timed, starting over if the banana is dropped, and the team with the shortest time wins.

6. *Doctor the Banana:* Each team is given a banana, a knife, and several toothpicks. Within an agreed time limit, each team performs Open Banana Surgery by carefully peeling the banana and slicing it into four equal pieces for a judge to verify the cuttings. Then, the patients are cured by using the toothpicks to put the banana back together again. The team with the most "cured" banana wins.

7. *Couples' Banana Eat:* Each team selects a couple to represent them. Place a peeled banana with one end in the boy's mouth and the other in the girl's. The first couple to eat the banana without using their hands wins.

8. *Banana-Eating Contest:* Couples face each other with a banana placed on a table between them. At a signal, they must peel and eat the banana without using their hands. They must do everything with their teeth. It's a riot to watch.

9. *Barbie Banana Beauty Contest:* All you need are a few naked bananas and some paper doll dress-up clothes (or pictures of clothes from magazines and catalogues). Each person dresses his banana to enter the beauty contest.

10. *All My Bananas:* Using their beauty contest bananas, the kids write three-minute soap operas. Then, teams compete for the most gripping dramatic presentation.

11. *Custom-Banana Hot Rod Show:* Give each team a model car kit to customize their banana to enter the Custom-Banana Hot Rod Show. If their banana car will roll, they enter the Banana Hot Rod Grand Prix. Let each team roll their cars down an incline. The champ is the one who reaches the bottom first or goes the farthest.

12. *Banana Videos:* Using video cameras, each group makes a real video with their banana puppets. The bananas can lip-sync their favorite record.

13. *Banana Air-Band Contest:* The kids lip-sync records using bananas as instruments. It's fun to watch this later, so you may want to video record this contest.

14. *Tip-Banana-Toe:* This game is messy, so play on a floor that is easily cleaned or outside. Line up chairs to create an aisle to be strewn with banana peels. Contestants are then blindfolded and must walk down the aisle without stepping on a banana peel. Chances are they won't make it.

15. *Banana Power Munching:* This is just a good old See-Who-Can-Eat-the-Most-Bananas-in-a-Certain-Period-of-Time Contest.

16. *Banana-Feet Relay:* Kids line up facing one direction, then sit down. The first person picks up the banana with his feet, rolls over straight-backed, then feets-off (hands-off) the banana to the next person, who takes it from that person's feet using only his own feet. The last person peels the banana and eats it. If in teams, the first to finish is the winner.

17. *Capture the Banana:* Play CAPTURE THE FLAG only use bananas.

You can invent your own banana games if you need more. There are many games that require balls—substitute bananas; relays require the passing of a baton—use bananas. For refreshments, what else? Banana Splits!

 A BLOW OUT!

The theme of this special event is *tires.* If you promote it properly, your kids will really get pumped for this one. When the kids arrive, divide into teams named Goodyears, UniRoyals, and Michelins. Then, play some of these wild games.

1. *Tire Relay:* Roll tires along a course with a person riding inside the tire.

2. *Inner-Tube Relay:* Teams pair off, and couples run to an inner tube and squeeze through it together. They pull the tube over their heads and push it down to their feet.

3. *Inner-Tube Pack:* See how many kids each team can get inside a large tractor tire tube (around the waists).

4. *Tire Scavenger Hunt:* Send the kids around the neighborhood to bring back as many old tires as they can in fifteen minutes.

5. *Tire Change:* Each team gets a car. They race to see which team can change a tire on all four wheels (rotate the tires).

6. *Tire Diving:* Hang a tire from a tree. See which team can dive through the tire in the fastest time.

7. *Tire Slalom:* Set up a slalom course and have the teams roll their tires along the course all at the same time. Turning sharp corners is not easy, and kids running their tires into each other makes this a crazy race.

8. *Tire Stack:* See which team can stack a pile of tires the highest.

9. *Tire Obstacle Course:* Arrange some tires flat on the ground side-by-side and the rest in a tire tunnel (tires set up in a row). Kids run relay-style through this obstacle course.

10. *Pit Crew Contest:* One contestant stands at the starting line. Eight tires are placed over his head and stacked. When all eight tires are stacked, he moves to the finish line, ten feet away. There the tires are unstacked one at a time. Continue play with several different people in the middle but keep the pit crew the same.

11. *Indy 500:* Each team selects a race car (four tires) and races them in position (front left, front right, rear left, rear right) around an oval track.

12. *Inner-Tube Soccer:* Play a regular game of soccer but use an inner tube, instead of a soccer ball.

13. *Tire Transfer:* Stack a bunch of tires at the starting line and mark the finish line, thirty feet away. The team to transfer and restack the tires the quickest wins.

14. *Tire Toss:* Kids compete to see who can throw a tire (or tube) the farthest.

15. *Tire Ball:* Place tires at different distances from a line behind which players toss softballs or bean-bags. The tires farther away are given higher point values. Each person gets the same number of tosses.

There are other games that can be played using tires and tubes. To add to the occasion, referees can dress up in mechanics garb and wave checkered flags at finish lines. Adapt this event to fit your own situation. Memorial Day weekend, when the annual Indy 500 takes place, is a good time to schedule this. For refreshments, serve donuts (tires) and cider (gasoline).

★ **COME-AS-YOU-WERE PARTY**

You've heard of a Come-As-You-Are Party. Well, this is a Come-As-You-*Were* Party. Everyone comes dressed like they were when they were a baby, such as wearing jammies with feet, diapers, or play clothes like a child would wear. They can bring dolls, baby bottles, blankets, pacifiers, or anything that makes them feel like a baby once again.

After everyone has arrived, play the following games.

1. *Best-Dressed Baby Contest:* Have judges select the best baby costume worn to the party.

2. *Baby-Picture Guessing:* Ask everyone to bring his baby picture to the party. Number them and have the kids try to match the pictures with their grown-up friends. Throw in a few extras to make it a little more difficult.

3. *Baby Buggy Race:* Get an old baby carriage or stroller for each team. Relay-style, each person pushes the carriage around a goal and back with one of his teammates riding in it.

4. *Bottle-Drinking Contest:* Fill a few baby bottles full of warm milk and have contestants compete to see who can drink his bottle in the fastest time.

5. *Diaper Change:* Give the girls some large diapers (ripped up sheets will work fine) and have them race to diaper the boys, or have the boys race to diaper a doll in the fastest time.

6. *Baby-Food Race:* The girls feed a jar of baby food to the guys. The first to finish is the winner.

7. *Baby-Crying Contest:* Have the kids compete to see who can cry the loudest, most dramatically, and most convincingly.

★ EGGSTRAVAGANZA

This special event would be good around Easter because its theme is *eggs*. Ask the kids to bring a dozen eggs as their price of admission, then play some of the following games.

1. *The Egg-and-Armpit Relay:* Team members carry a raw egg under their armpit around a goal and back.

2. *The Egg Toss:* Team members stand about three feet apart and play catch with a raw egg. On each toss, they take one step backward, getting farther and farther away. When they miss, they are eliminated.

3. *The Egg-and-Spoon Relay:* Team members carry a raw egg around a goal and back on a spoon.

4. *Egg Golf:* Set up a miniature golf course around the room with pieces of paper marked as holes. Kids try to golf the egg with their shoes. Eggs can be raw or hard-boiled.

5. *The Egg Drop:* Boy-girl couples compete. Guys lie down on the floor and hold a paper cup in their mouths. The girls stand on a chair, crack a raw egg, and try to drop the contents of the egg into the cup. Whoever gets the most egg in the cup wins.

6. *Egg-Decorating Contest:* Furnish art supplies and have the kids compete in an egg-decorating contest. They can try to decorate eggs to look like famous people or people in the church. Judges award prizes for the best.

7. *Egghead Contest:* Almost any quiz could be used to determine who is the Egghead of the group.

8. *Egg Chugalug:* See who can eat the most raw eggs.

For refreshments, serve egg salad sandwiches, quiche, fried chicken, or anything with eggs in it. Be creative and you won't ''lay an egg'' with these activities.

★ FANTASY ISLAND NIGHT

This special event is based on the old television show of the same name, but it doesn't have to be. Invite everyone to come to a party dressed in costumes that represent their *fantasy*—a particular role or career in life they would like to achieve or a contemporary celebrity or historical figure they would like to be or be like.

After everyone has arrived, each person tells about his fantasy. Later in the evening award prizes for categories, such as Most Imaginative and Creative, The Reachable Star, The Impossible Dream, and The Weirdest. If you use the Fantasy Island theme, ask someone to dress as Mr. Rourke and another person as Tattoo to be hosts for the evening. Decorations and refreshments can have an island theme.

★ FOOT PARTY

Here's a great way, literally, to kick off the new year. Plan an event with a *feet* theme. Everyone comes to the party barefoot. Absolutely no shoes allowed. Divide into teams with names, like the Toe Jams, Bunions, and Hangnails. Then, play some of the following feet games.

1. *Foot-Painting Contest:* Give teams some newsprint and have them paint pictures with their feet. They can use brushes or do toe painting (finger painting with toes).

2. *Foot Awards:* Award points and prizes for the largest foot, the smallest foot, the ugliest foot, the funniest-looking foot, and the smelliest foot.

3. *Foot Footage:* Teams line up with their feet toe-to-heel. The team with the longest combined length wins.

4. *Foot Signing:* This is a good mixer. Kids see how many autographs they can get on the bottoms of their feet.

5. *Foot Wrestling:* Kids sit on the floor facing each other. They lock toes and try to pin the other person's foot, similar to arm wrestling.

6. *Lemon Pass:* Teams line up and sit on the floor, then try to pass a lemon along the line and back using only their feet. The lemon cannot touch the floor.

7. *Foot Scramble:* Paint letters on the bottom of kids' feet. Each team has the same letters. Then, shout words that contain those letters. The kids with those letters on their feet must sit down in a row and arrange their feet in order, so the word can be read by the judges. To make this more challenging, one kid has two different letters on each of his feet and both of those letters are needed in the word.

Be imaginative and invent many other games to use the feet theme. For refreshments—how about foot-long hot dogs?

★ FRISBEE FROLICK

Here is a good daytime event, incorporating those famous *flying discs*, which are so popular with kids. Have kids bring their own Frisbees and frolick with some of these games.

1. *Distance Frisbee:* Line up teams in columns behind a line. Each player tosses the Frisbee three times for distance. After each person throws, a judge marks the spot. The thrower retrieves the Frisbee for the next person in line. Prizes can be given for the farthest throw and the first team to finish.

2. *Accuracy Frisbee:* Teams are lined up, and a tire or a cardboard box is placed about twenty-five feet away. Team members toss the Frisbee through the tire or into the box. The team with the highest total of successful tosses is the winner.

3. *Team-Toss Frisbee:* Two teams line up opposite each other about twenty feet apart. The first person on one team throws the Frisbee to the first person on the other team, who tosses it back to the second person on the first team, who throws it back to the second person on the second team, and so on. The thrower's team scores a point if the catcher drops the Frisbee, and the catcher's team scores a point if the thrower tosses the Frisbee beyond the reach of the catcher, who must keep his feet planted. There should be a judge to rule in close calls.

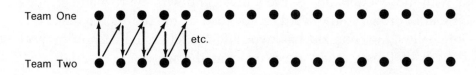

4. *Crazy Legs Frisbee:* Teams line up in columns behind a starting line, and a finish line is placed about twenty feet away. Each team has one Frisbee. The first person places the Frisbee between his knees and runs to the finish line where he tosses the Frisbee back to the next person in line.

5. *Frisbee Water Brigade:* Teams line up and one-by-one carry water in the Frisbee from a water source to an empty container about thirty feet away. First team to fill the container with water wins.

6. *Frisbee Stand-Off:* You will need one expendable Frisbee for this one. The object is to get as many people as possible on the Frisbee either with their feet partially or wholly on the Frisbee or with their weight completely supported by people who are standing on the Frisbee. Give each team a couple of minutes to practice, then see which team can do the best job.

7. *Frisbee Distance Relay:* You need a lot of room for this relay (maybe a deserted road). The first person on each team throws a Frisbee for distance. The second person picks up the Frisbee where it landed and throws it again in the same direction, and so on. Whichever team gets the Frisbee the farthest distance away from the starting point wins.

8. *Frisbee Golf:* Set up a golf course, using cardboard boxes for holes. Play golf with the Frisbees. Each toss of the Frisbee is like a golf swing, teeing off at each hole and taking the next swing from wherever the Frisbee lands. Determine par ahead of time. To add excitement, include some water hazards, dog legs, and other obstacles to toss around.

9. *Frisbee Freestyle:* This is for all the "hot dogs" in the group. You can have one or two participants from each team demonstrate their best freestyle Frisbee throw—around the back, under the leg, over the head, double skip, boomerang, or any other kind of fancy or crazy shot. A panel of distinguished and expert judges can determine the winners.

At the conclusion of the event, award prizes and serve refreshments. You might purchase a quantity of mini-Frisbees and use them as plates.

GARBAGE-IN, GARBAGE-OUT PARTY

Here's one that many of your kids will be able to relate to with ease. You could also call it a Trash Bash and get the same results. The theme is *trash, garbage, junk, and rubbish.* Ask the kids to come dressed in their very worst clothes and try these games.

1. *Garbage Bobbing:* This one bears a striking resemblance to Bobbing for Apples, but the object is slightly different. Award points for various kinds of garbage retrieved with the teeth from the tub of floating goodies.

2. *Trash Scavenger Hunt:* Send the kids out with a list of stuff that has been, is going to be, or should have been discarded.

3. *A Bigger and Worser Hunt:* You could do this instead of the Trash Scavenger Hunt. Teams start with some item of trash, and run around the neighborhood trying to trade down for something worse at each house. The team that returns with the worst trash is the winner.

4. *Garbage-Bag Volleyball:* Actually, there are lots of games that can be played with those big plastic bags. Fill one up with air, tie it off, and use it as a volleyball.

5. *Musical Garbage:* Put some leftover garbage in a bag and pass it around the room as the music plays. When the music stops, whoever is holding it must eat it, or have it dumped on his head, or . . . ?

For refreshments, make punch out of watered-down lemonade with orange peels, lemon peels, apples, peppers, celery, and other "garbage" floating around in it and serve it from a (clean) garbage can. Ask parents to provide plenty of leftovers for refreshments. Be creative, and you can make this the absolute awfullest event of the year!

★ HALLELUJAH HOEDOWN

Depending on where you live, your young people may enjoy an event centered around the theme of *hillbillies,* especially effective if combined with a real, old-fashioned hayride. Activities could include the following:

1. *Hillbilly Fashion Show:* Have the kids come dressed as hillbillies and award prizes to the best-dressed hillbillies.

2. *The Corn-fusion Game:* This is like the old game of Confusion, where you give kids a list of about eight things they have to do in any order they wish. Create your own game but give it a hillbilly theme. Here are some samples.

Find someone who has used a real outhouse and have them initial here: _____

Get three people together and call hogs for ten seconds as loudly as you can. One of them initials here: _____

Find someone to be a plow. You hold their legs while they walk on their hands. Plow a furrow about ten feet long. They initial here: _____

3. *The Barnyard Game:* Secretly assign everyone the name of a barnyard animal. Turn off the lights, and everyone mingles around the room making the sound of his animal. All those making the same sound get together and lock arms. The group that finds the most members is the winner. For fun, assign one person the donkey.

4. *Hillbilly Talent Competition:* Have the kids come prepared to compete for prizes. Talent must be authentic hillbilly talent, such as banjo picking, yodeling, cow chip tossing, hog calling, nose singing, knee slapping, and spitting.

Plan a Bar-B-Q and serve good country vittles—mashed potatoes and biscuits, black-eyed peas, corn-on-the-cob, and a few freezers of homemade ice cream ready to crank. Decorate with a country motif and provide some country or bluegrass music for atmosphere. Sometimes an event like this actually is most popular with kids who live in the city because it's a good change of pace.

★ A HOGWASH

Here's a good outdoor special event designed around *pigs*. You will need to borrow some real pigs from a nearby farm or school and cage them. Then, get your group together for an afternoon or evening of pig games.

1. *Name-That-Pig Contest:* If you have one pig for each team, let each team name their pig. Have a panel of judges pick the best-named pig.

2. *Pig-Decorating Contest:* Provide shaving cream, hats, ribbons, and clothes and let each team decorate their pig. A variation of this would be to have a Miss Piggy Contest and see which group can make their pig look the most like the famous Muppet. Award prizes for the best-decorated pig.

3. *Pickled-Pigs-Feet-Eating Contest:* Buy this delicacy at a grocery store and have one person from each team compete.

4. *Pig-Washing Contest:* This is the actual Hogwash part of the event. Give each team some soap, talcum powder, and deodorant. Judge the cleanest pig.

5. *Tail Tie:* With all the pigs in the pen, each team has one of their players locate their pig, chase it, and tie a ribbon on its tail. First to do so wins.

6. *Pig-Pen Contest:* Have each team select one person on their team to be Pig Pen, the "Peanuts" character. The rest of the team tries to decorate that person so he looks as dirty as possible. They can use mud, old rags, or charcoal.

7. *Hog-Calling Contest:* Put the pigs in a circle and have the teams call their pig. The team whose pig responds in the fastest time wins.

8. *Mud Fight:* Dig a mud hole and have one-minute mud fights. When it's all over, the cleanest team is the winner.

For refreshments, serve Prodigal Sundaes, named for one of history's first Hogwash participants. Make a V-shaped pig trough out of wood and line it with tin foil, then put the ice cream and toppings in the trough. The kids eat without using their hands, so they can make pigs out of themselves and "pig out."

★ **HULA HOOPLA**

This event makes good use of those popular *plastic hoops*, which have been around for years. Divide into teams and give each team a hula hoop for these games.

1. *Hula-Hoop Pack:* See which team can get the most kids inside the hula hoop, with the hoop around everyone's waist.

2. *Hula-Hoop Race:* Four kids from each team get inside a hula hoop and run around a goal and back. The hoop is then passed to the next four kids, and so on. This game is even more fun with six or seven kids inside the hoop.

3. *Hula Relay:* Teams line up relay-style. The first person puts the hoop around his waist and hulas around the goal and back, keeping the hoop up the whole time. Hands are not allowed.

4. *Hula Relay #2:* The hoop is placed about twenty feet away from the team. Each person runs to the hoop, picks it up, hulas ten times, drops the hoop, runs back to the team, and tags the next player.

5. *Jump-Through-the-Hoop Race:* Teams line up with two people holding the hoop vertically in front of the teams. At a signal, the players run through the hoop and go back to the end of the line. The team to get the most people through the hoop in sixty seconds wins.

There are other variations, such as tossing hula hoops like Frisbees, rolling them, or using them as targets. Hula-hoop games can be combined with a Hawaiian Luau theme for refreshments.

★ **A JELL-O RIOT**

How about an evening of *Jell-O* games?

1. *Jell-O-Ad Relay:* Get several newspapers that are all the same issue and contain plenty of grocery store advertisements. Go through the paper and find all the ads for Jell-O brand products. Cut them out and put them on display. Then, the teams try to find those ads in their paper in as short a time as possible to be the winner.

2. *Jell-O-Pie-Eating Contest:* Fill pie tins with Jell-O, cover with whipped cream, and have a good, old-fashioned pie-eating contest—no hands please.

3. *Nailing-Jell-O-to-a-Tree Contest:* Make Jell-O in 8″ by 8″ cake pans, about one-half inch thick. Let it cool. About one and a half hours ahead of the game, take it out of the refrigerator and place it in the freezer. When ready to play, take it out and cut it into one-inch squares. Give the teams nails and let them nail their Jell-O to a tree (log). The team that nails the most in one minute wins.

4. *Jell-O-and-Spoon Relay:* Give each team a spoon and a chunk of Jell-O that must be carried to a goal and back on the spoon.

5. *The Jell-O Gauntlet:* A path is laid out on the floor, and everyone lines up along both sides of the path. Pieces of Jell-O are placed in the path as obstacles. Contestants are blindfolded and must walk down the path with bare feet. Teammates can shout directions and warnings; opposing teammates can shout instructions to confuse them.

6. *Jell-O Tennis:* A chunk of Jell-O is placed on a tennis (or racquetball) racquet. Team members try to keep the Jell-O from falling through the racquet as it is passed from one person to the next in a relay.

7. *Jell-O Carving:* Give the kids chunks of Jell-O to carve into Jell-O sculptures. Award a prize for the best.

★ **LIFESAVER TOURNAMENT**

With a little creativity, you can also build a very successful event around the theme of *lifesavers*. Have everyone bring a roll of their favorite flavor, then play games like these:

1. *Ring Toss:* Construct two ring toss pegs by nailing a long, thin nail through a small, wooden base. Kids then toss lifesavers onto the nail for points or play like horseshoes.

2. *Distance Roll or Holy Roller:* See who can roll a lifesaver along the ground, on its edge, the farthest.

3. *Lifesaver Shuffleboard:* Draw a shuffleboard court (follow diagram on next page) on a tabletop or on the ground and make some small pushers out of sticks. Play regular shuffleboard.

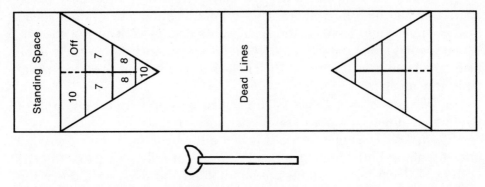

4. *Guess-the-Flavor Relay:* Put some lifesavers in a bag and have the teams line up relay-style. Each team member crawls to the bag blindfolded and takes out or is handed one lifesaver. He guesses its color by tasting, only one guess. If wrong, he goes back and tries again. Each person on the team must do this.

5. *Broom Hockey:* Play regular indoor Broom Hockey, using a lifesaver as a puck and brooms as hockey sticks.

6. *Lifesaver Barnyard:* Here's another variation of the Barnyard Game. Give everyone in the room different-colored lifesavers, so they are distributed evenly. Then have the kids suck on the lifesavers or just place them on their tongues. Without speaking, they must mill around the room and find others who have the same color on their tongues. The first group to get together is the winner.

In addition to these games, kids can make Lifesaver Jewelry or Lifesaver Hot Rods. For refreshments, serve lifesaver sundaes, lifesaver milk shakes, or lifesaver cookies.

★ **MARSHMALLOW TOURNAMENT**

Like the Lifesaver Tournament, this event features a kind of food—the *marshmallow*. There are all kinds of things you can do with a marshmallow to have fun, so plan an evening of marshmallow activities like these:

1. *Marshmallow Creations:* Give the kids some marshmallows and toothpicks and have them create sculptures. Judges decide the winners.

2. *Accuracy Throw:* Each person gets a marshmallow and tries to toss it into a basket some distance away. When a person misses, he's out. The last one to stay in the game is the winner.

3. *Distance Throw:* See who can throw a marshmallow the farthest. If space is limited, have a marshmallow shot put.

4. *Marshmallow Catch:* Couples stand a certain distance apart and toss the marshmallow back and forth, each time taking a step backward. If they miss the catch, they're out.

5. *Marshmallow Bagging:* This game is a lot of fun. Have the kids form a circle, so each person is about four feet apart. Determine a beginning point in the circle and place two bags at that point—a bag full of marshmallows and an empty bag. At a signal, the person by the full bag takes out one marshmallow and tosses it to the next person in the circle, who tosses it to the next person until the person next to the empty bag drops the marshmallow into the bag. The team to get the most marshmallows into the empty bag in sixty seconds is the winner. For an interesting twist to this game, have someone from another team sit by the empty bag, and as the marshmallows are fed into the bag, he eats them as fast as he can. He can only pull them out one at a time with one hand. A fast eater can keep a team's score pretty low.

6. *Bobbing for Marshmallows:* Kids bob for marshmallows, floating in chocolate syrup.

7. *Marshmallow Pitch:* Have couples get about ten feet apart, facing each other. One person (the pitcher) gets a sack of marshmallows (any size) and tosses them to his partner, who must catch them in his mouth.

8. *Porky Mallow:* Have the teams or the group line up in a single-file line. Give everyone a toothpick (round ones work best). All players hold their toothpicks in their teeth. The first person in line sticks a marshmallow on the end of his toothpick and passes it to the next person, who stabs it with his toothpick. The first person leaves his toothpick in the marshmallow, so as it collects more and more toothpicks, it becomes increasingly difficult to pass.

9. *Marshmallow Golf:* Get some plastic putting cups from a sports store and a few golf putters. Then, lay out a course around the church, using steps, corridors, and barriers. The ball is a slightly stale marshmallow and because of its shape, will take some very interesting rolls.

10. *The 40-Inch Dash:* Have three or four contestants compete in this little contest. Each person gets a marshmallow with a forty-inch piece of string attached to it. They put the loose end of the string in their mouths, so the marshmallow hangs straight down toward the floor. At a signal, the players chew their strings to get the marshmallows into their mouths without using their hands. Their teammates can cheer them on.

11. *Marshmallow Drop:* Have kids pair off, with one person lying on the floor and the other standing next to him. The person who is standing gets three marshmallows and a cup of chocolate syrup. He dips the marshmallow in the chocolate, then drops the marshmallow into the other person's mouth. Award a prize for three successful catches.

Ask the kids to wear marshmallow colors and bring a bag of marshmallows for admission. Later, everyone makes the refreshments. Each person gets two graham crackers, a half-piece of a Hershey bar, and a marshmallow. The marshmallow is roasted over a fire, then placed between the graham crackers with the Hershey bar—S'mores.

★ **NERF FESTIVAL**

There is available a wide assortment of *Nerf* balls and toys. Collect a variety of these to have a Nerf Festival. Invite all of the kids to bring their Nerf toys, although you may want to purchase a few of your own. Organize different kinds of ball games, such as football-passing contests and relays. For refreshments, serve sponge cake.

★ **NEWSPAPER NIGHT**

Here's a good special event built around the theme of *newspapers.* To prepare for it, collect a huge pile of old newspapers, the more the better. This event could be combined with a newspaper drive. Perhaps the paper collection can take place during the day, and then in the evening, you can play some of the following games.

1. *Newspaper Costume Race:* Teams have five minutes to dress kids with newspapers to look like certain characters, for example: Santa Claus or Abraham Lincoln.

2. *Newspaper Treasure Hunt:* Give each team a pile of newspapers with some special slips of paper hidden in them. The first team to find them all is the winner.

3. *Newspaper Scavenger Hunt:* Call out certain items from the papers, for example, an advertisement for Chevrolet, a news item about a murder, or a baseball box score. The first team to find them wins.

4. *Wad-and-Pile Contest:* Teams get ten minutes to wad up all their paper into a big pile. The highest pile wins.

5. *Hide-and-Seek:* Hide as many kids as possible under the pile of wadded-up newspapers. The team with the most kids under the paper and out-of-sight is the winner.

6. *Compact Newspapers:* Teams try to compact their pile of paper into as small a pile as possible.

7. *Snowball Fight:* Make a line of chairs between the two teams. Teams are given time to wad up all their paper into snowballs. At a signal, they throw as much of their snow as possible over to the other team's side. When the whistle blows, everyone stops. The team with the least amount of paper on their side is the winner.

8. *Disposal Event:* Give every team plastic trash bags. Make a contest out of putting all the newspaper (trash) into the bags. The team that fills the most bags is the winner.

★ A NIGHT IN THE TROPICS

Here's a good way to take boredom out of the winter months, especially if you live in a cold climate. Plan a "tropical" party on a South Pacific island for a night. Decorations should include posters of Hawaii and Tahiti (available from a travel agency), fish nets on the wall, potted green plants and palms (borrow them from a nursery), sea shells, wicker chairs, and tropical fish. Background music should be Hawaiian or steel-band music, such as that of Don Ho, Arthur Lyman, or the Beach Boys.

An extra attraction might be a tanning beach, with lights that simulate the sun's ultraviolet rays. Provide suntan lotion.

On the invitations, ask kids to dress appropriately—shorts, aloha shirts, muu-muus, sandals, beachcomber hats, and puka-shell necklaces. Have some extras for kids who cannot find anything to wear. When the kids arrive, give them a flower lei (paper or real) and play some appropriate games, such as a Hula-dancing Contest, the Limbo Walk (walking with only knees bent under a stick that is lowered with each try), and Click-Clacks (dancing between sticks held just above the floor as they are clicked together and on the floor rhythmically).

For refreshments, create a giant fruit tray, tropical punch bowl, and other appropriate goodies, like fried bananas, coconut granola, and pineapple slices. You might want to plan a luau, complete with barbecued pork, rice, and all the trimmings. Conclude the evening with some music, skits, or a film that features surfing and water sports. In the middle of January, this event is quite popular.

★ NOISE NIGHT

Now kids can really let off some steam. For a change, they will have a legitimate excuse to make as much *noise* as they possibly can. You will, of course, want to make sure you hold this event where neighbors won't get upset. Here are some suggested activities.

1. *Screaming Contest:* Set up a microphone to a tape recorder with needles and lights that monitor the volume. Each kid (or team) stands about twenty feet away from the microphone and makes as loud a noise as possible using his mouth only (no clapping or other such noises). See who can register the loudest scream.

2. *Identify the Noise:* In advance of the event, make a tape recording of a variety of noises and ask the kids to identify them.

3. *Noise Scavenger Hunt:* Divide into teams and give each team a tape recorder and a list of noises they have to find and record, such as a diesel horn or a dog barking.

4. *Yeller Relay:* Team members try to yell instructions to each other from a distance of about twenty feet. At the same time, the opposing team makes as much distracting and contradictory noise as possible. For example, the first person runs to a point away from the team and receives an instruction, "Run with your right hand over your head." He must yell that instruction to the next person in line until that person understands and follows the instruction, while the opposing team members are trying to prevent the person from hearing it. Both teams play at the same time.

5. *Noise Contest:* Divide into teams, and each team tries to make the most obnoxious, disgusting noise they possibly can. Judges determine the winner.

6. *Cap Smash:* Get a hammer and a roll of caps (toy pistol ones) for each person, who sees how many caps he can set off while the group counts for ten seconds. This game is even more fun when the contestants are blindfolded.

When you advertise this event, always yell the announcements at the group as loudly as you can with a lot of background noise, like rock music or static. At the event, tell the group that any time they say anything to anyone else, they must yell it as loudly as they can. Give a prize at the end of the event for whoever is the hoarsest or loses his voice. For refreshments, how about some "ice-scream"?

★ **NOSTALGIA NIGHT**

This is a special event or party idea, which can take many different forms. The idea is simply to *go back in time* for one night. You could make it an 1890's Night, a Roaring 20's Night, a 50's Night, or any other period of time you choose; however, be certain the time period lends itself easily to getting costumes, music, decorations, and refreshments. Have everyone come dressed in period clothing, decorate the room appropriately with antiques, play music from the period (dance to it?), and show some old-time movies. Award prizes for the best-dressed, most authentic costumes. For added fun, take the whole group in their costumes to an ice-cream parlor or some other restaurant of the chosen time period for refreshments.

★ ONCE-A-YEAR BIRTHDAY PARTY

The theme of this event is *birthdays*. Its purpose is to celebrate everyone's birthday all at once. Arrange twelve tables and decorate each according to the events of that particular month of the year. Make a birthday cake for each month and set it at the appropriate table, along with ice cream to be served later, and party favors, like hats, party blowers, and streamers.

Play a variety of traditional birthday party games—Pin the Tail on the Donkey and Drop the Clothespin in the Milk Bottle. Then, play a few of these other birthday games.

1. *Birthday Barnyard:* As the kids come in, have them mill around the room making a sound that corresponds to the month or group of months they were born in. They must find others making the same sound and get into birthday groups. Here are some sample sounds.

January–February	Brrrrrr
March–April	(Make the sound of wind blowing)
May–June	Hum "Here Comes the Bride" or "Pomp and Circumstance"
July–August	Whoopee!
September–October	Boo!
November–December	Ho-ho-ho!

2. *Birthday Scramble:* Divide into two teams. At a signal, kids must line up in the order of their birthdays. First team to get in the correct order is the winner.

3. *Gift-Wrapping Contest:* Give teams something that is difficult to gift-wrap, then have them compete to see who can do the best, most creative job. To really make this interesting, have them gift-wrap a live duck.

4. *Birthday Cheers:* Group the kids according to birthday months. Then each birthday group creates and gives cheers for their particular month. Judges pick the best cheers and award prizes or birthday gifts to the winners.

After each person is sitting at his birthday table, the program can include awards for the oldest person, the youngest, the person with a birthday on a holiday, the person who was born farthest away from where you live, the person who most recently had a birthday, and the next person to have a birthday. It's a great way to honor everyone's birthday at one big special event.

★ **PIT PARTY**

This special event can be promoted as really being *the pits.* Tell the kids they can come looking like the pits, if they want. Here are some sample activities.

1. *Pit Pass:* Team members attempt to pass a Nerf ball (or similar object) from person to person using only their armpits. A variation is a relay where kids carry an object (a raw egg or a water balloon) around a goal and back in their armpits.

2. *Pit Stop:* This relay game requires each team member to stop halfway on the race course for a pit stop, where he eats or drinks something before continuing the race.

3. *Pit Skits:* Have the group divide into teams and create short skits with the theme "It's the pits." Give each team a sack of items to incorporate into the skit or tell them the last line of their skit must be "Boy, is this the pits!" Judges can determine the winning skits.

4. *Giant Pit:* The popular table game Pit can be adapted into a group game with a few alterations. If you have the game, play it by teams, rather than by individuals.

5. *Pit-Guessing Contest:* Collect an assortment of pits from different fruits. Kids guess which fruit they come from.

6. *Pit Shooting:* Kids shoot wet fruit pits for accuracy by squeezing them between their fingers.

Brainstorm some additional ideas with your kids. For refreshments, serve some different kinds of pitted food, like cherries, plums, apricots, prunes, olives, and peaches. For prizes, some underarm deodorant would be fitting.

★ **PRISON PARTY**

Here's a special event with a *jailhouse* theme. Decorate a gym or large room in a prison decor with bars on the windows and a siren handy for crowd control. The youth sponsors dress like prison guards. When the kids arrive, have some police officers arrest them, fingerprint them, frisk them, and book them into the prison. Give each person an identification number and take mug shots. Then, play some of these prison games.

1. *The Ball-and-Chain Stomp:* This is the Balloon Stomp game with a new name. Tie balloons around each person's ankles. He tries to stomp and pop other prisoners' balloons, keeping his own from getting stomped. Whoever lasts the longest wins.

2. *The Tunnel Escape:* Make a tunnel out of cardboard boxes and tables. Divide into teams and see how many cellmates can escape to freedom within a given time limit. Teams line up at one end of the tunnel and crawl through one at a time as quickly as they can, then return to the end of the line, and go through again, if they can.

3. *Murder in Cell Block Five:* One person is secretly designated as the murderer. The lights go out, and that person walks around the room while everyone else is milling about and whispers in someone's ear, "You're dead." Whoever gets that message counts to ten, dies, and is out of the game. If someone wants to try and guess who the murderer is, he can take an official guess, but if wrong, he is also dead. The object is for the murderer to knock off as many victims as possible before being discovered.

4. *Breakout:* Play this game outside in the parking lot if it is a really dark night. Set up a guard tower that can hold a couple of people. Two kids are chosen to be guards and are given powerful flashlights. A bell is placed underneath the guard tower. At a signal, the rest of the kids try to sneak up to the guard tower and ring the bell without getting shot with the flashlight. As soon as someone successfully rings the bell, he trades places with one of the guards. Judges can decide close calls.

5. *Find the Loot:* This game is similar to Hunters and Hounds. Divide into teams with each team choosing a captain. The object is for each team to find as much loot as possible. The loot can be play money, which has been hidden ahead of time by the sponsors. If you are using a church, then the loot can be hidden in classrooms, trees, desks, or trash cans. At a signal, the teams look for the loot, but the team captains must stay in a central waiting area. As soon as a team member finds some loot, he must run back and tell his team captain where it is. The team captain gets the loot himself—no one else may touch it—and returns to the waiting area before being allowed to go after more loot.

6. *Exercise Yard:* Play almost any kind of relay or team game.

If possible, provide the kids with some kind of prison uniform (hats and T-shirts) and serve refreshments in the mess hall. This event could introduce or complete a presentation and discussion about freedom, justice and the prison system, or a field trip to a jail or rehabilitation center.

★ CRAZY REVIVAL!

If your church is planning some special church services in the future, here's a special event that will generate some excitement and enthusiasm with your kids. When the kids arrive, tell them that to know how to attend a church service, they need to practice certain church-going skills. Then, play some of these games.

1. *Find a Seat:* Just in case there is a standing-room-only crowd at the next church service, they better practice getting a seat. Play Musical Chairs.

2. *Pass the Plate:* It takes skill to pass the offering plate! Play any relay game, but use an offering plate as the baton to pass.

3. *Grab the Hymnal:* There aren't always enough hymnals to go around, so you've got to be quick. Play Steal the Bacon with an old hymnbook.

4. *Name That Hymn:* It's time to sing! Play charades with titles of hymns. As soon as the guessing team knows the name of the hymn, they must sing a few bars.

5. *Memory Verse:* This is practice for listening to the reading of the Scripture for the day. Play the Gossip game, using a verse of Scripture.

Kids line up, and the verse is whispered in the ear of the first person, who whispers it to the second, and so on. The last person must quote the verse correctly.

5. *Sermon Cheers:* Kids need to practice responding to good points in the sermon. Distribute slips of paper with words and phrases, like Amen!, Hallelujah!, Preach it, brother!, and Glory! At a signal, everyone mills around and shouts his word or phrase, trying to find others shouting the same thing. The first group to get everyone together is the winner.

 SMALL WORLD PARTY

Here's a special event that is not only a lot of fun but will also help increase *world awareness* among members of your group. Advertise it as a Small World Party and give all the activities an international flavor. Kids should wear clothing and costumes from other countries. Here are some examples.

1. *Name-Tag Mixer:* When each person arrives, have him make a name tag representing his family's original nationality. If some kids don't know, let them choose any nationality they wish. Emphasize creativity. Allow fifteen to twenty minutes and award prizes for the most unusual or most creative.

2. *Signature Mixer:* Give everyone a list of about twenty items, similar to the sample list here, which is specific for your group. The kids need a signature for each item.

Someone who was born out of the U.S.: _____

Someone who has lived in another country: _____

Someone who likes Chinese food: _____

Someone who can speak Spanish: _____

3. *Costume Fashion Show:* Those who wore international costumes model them, and judges choose the most elaborate, the most creative, and the funniest.

4. *Folk Games:* Go to your local library and find books of games from other countries. Perhaps you can find a few people who are familiar with popular folk games from other countries who would be willing to lead them. Play as many as time permits.

An event like this can be a lot of fun if no one views it too seriously. Combine it with an International Progressive Dinner or serve foods and snacks from different countries, such as Swedish meatballs, nachos and guacamole dip, and little pizzas. During a missions emphasis at your church, this special event provides a good backdrop.

★ **TATOR NIGHT**

Here's a fun special event centered around the theme of *potatoes.* Advertise it with slogans, such as Don't be a Vegi-Tator or a Hesi-Tator . . . Come to Tator Night! Get some potato sacks and make shirts out of them for everyone. Ask everyone to bring a few potatoes as their admission. Give an award to whoever brings the biggest potato, the ugliest potato, and the most beautiful potato. Then, play some of these potato games.

1. *Tator Contest:* Have a Tator-tasting Contest, using several different brands of potato chips (you can usually find at least a dozen different brands in local supermarkets). To make a contest, place the chips in numbered bowls and see if the kids can match up the chips with the brand name. As a variation, use French fries from various fast-food restaurants around town.

2. *The People's Tator:* This skit is a take-off on the television show "The People's Court." You will need twelve different people to play the Tator Family (members of the jury), listed below, and one person to be Judge Tator. Each Tator Family member must respond to questions in such a way to reveal his personality. As the jury is asked questions by Judge Tator, the rest of the group tries to guess what personality each Tator Family member is exhibiting. Afterward, reveal the Tator names.

Speck-Tator	Dick-Tator	Agi-Tator
Hesi-Tator	Emmy-Tator	Cogi-Tator
Common-Tator	Irri-Tator	Vegi-Tator
Devis-Tator	Facili-Tator	Medi-Tator

3. *Mr. Potato-Head Race:* Divide the group into teams, the number of teams being equivalent to the Mr. Potato Head games you have available (check your local toy store). The object of the game is for each team to put together their Mr. Potato Head successfully. Teams line up single file about twenty feet from Mr. Potato Head, and each person runs to him blindfolded and adds one more part. The first team to finish or whichever team has the best-looking Mr. Potato Head at the end of the time limit is the winner.

4. *Baked-Potatoes Scramble:* Write on a blackboard or a large piece of butcher paper the words "baked potatoes." Have the kids pair off and see which pair can come up with the most words using only the letters in these words. Each letter can be used only as many times as it appears in these two words.

5. *Potato Push:* Kids push a potato along the ground in a figure-eight course, using only their heads (noses, chins, foreheads). Give each person a potato and let them all push together. It's really fun to watch.

All sorts of ball games and relays can also be played with potatoes, like potato football. Divide the group into teams using potato names, such as the Russets, the Idahos, the Scallops, and the Hash Browns. Serve gourmet baked potatoes for a delicious way to end (or begin) the evening.

★ **TURTLE TOURNAMENT**

For this special event, you'll need live *turtles*, preferably large ones. One turtle for every four kids constitutes a turtle team. Turtle events can include the following:

1. *Turtle-Decorating Contest:* Provide paint, dye, paper, and ribbon. Each team decorates their turtle for judging.

2. *Turtle Races:* Draw concentric circles on the ground with the largest about fifteen feet in diameter. Place the turtles in the center (the smallest circle), and they may "run" in any direction. The turtle to go the farthest in the time limit is the winner.

3. *Turtle Tricks:* Each team is given ten minutes to teach, train, or force their turtle to do a "trick." Props may be used, and judges give points for creativity, ingenuity, and turtle talent.

4. *Turtle Chariot Races:* Each team is given cardboard, paper, tape, and wheels to construct a chariot for their turtle to pull. Judge for the best chariots, then have a race.

Make sure the kids do not abuse the turtles. Have each team name their turtle and keep a tote board with the team names. To add to the derby atmosphere, have a starting gun and checkered flags. This special event is different enough to be a lot of fun.

★ **WATERMELON OLYMPICS**

This special event would be good for a summertime family event. Ask each family to bring a watermelon and a picnic lunch, then play a variety of watermelon games.

1. *Watermelon Grab:* Hide all the watermelons, like eggs for an Easter egg hunt, then divide into two groups—the grabbers and the taggers. The grabbers try to locate and bring a watermelon to home base without being tagged by the taggers. If tagged, they must put the watermelon down on the spot where they were tagged and go to jail. Grabbers can only be tagged while carrying a watermelon. See how many watermelons can be successfully brought to home base within a given time limit, then switch sides.

2. *Watermelon Sack Race:* Play this like a regular sack race, only the contestants must carry a watermelon as they hop along with both feet in the sack.

3. *Watermelon Balance:* Each team is given a watermelon and a tennis racquet. Players must carry the watermelon on the head of the racket to a goal and back, not touching the watermelon with any part of their bodies.

4. *Speed Seed-Eating-and-Spitting Contest:* Cut the watermelons into wedges and place them on a table. Give each team a styrofoam cup. At a signal, teams start eating watermelon and spitting their seeds into the cup. The first team to fill up their cup with seeds is the winner.

5. *Watermelon Rolling:* In this relay, participants roll a watermelon around a figure-eight course.

6. *Watermelon Carving:* Have a contest to see who can carve the most creative designs out of the watermelon rinds.

7. *Seed Target-Shooting:* Watermelon seeds can be shot quite a distance by squeezing them with the fingers. Set up targets and see who can be most accurate.

★ WHEELBARROW OLYMPICS

These Olympics are centered around *wheelbarrows*. Divide the group into equal teams of eight to ten. Each team should have a wheelbarrow. Try to obtain well-built wheelbarrows that are equally matched in size and weight (contractors' wheelbarrows are best). For safety, these wheelbarrow games should be played on a grassy area.

1. *Wheelbarrow Relay:* Teams line up and team members pair off, so one person rides in the wheelbarrow and the other pushes. At the starting signal, the wheelbarrow and rider are pushed to a marker about twenty-five feet away, then trade places, so the rider becomes the pusher and vice versa. The next two team members continue the game.

2. *Wheelbarrow-Tube Race:* This relay, similar to the preceding one, has an automobile-sized inner tube at the marker, and the players must squeeze through the tube together before returning to the team.

3. *Wheelbarrow Jousting:* Draw a circle (with chalk powder or a rope) about fifteen to twenty feet in diameter. Two guys from each team get in the circle with a wheelbarrow, one pushing and one riding on his knees. The object is to remain in the circle and upset the opposition. Riders cannot touch either wheelbarrow but can touch each other and the pushers; however, no hitting or using fists is allowed. If wheelbarrows touch, they are out. The last wheelbarrow to remain in the circle is the winner.

4. *Three-Man Relay:* Three members of each team compete at the same time with a wheelbarrow. One person rides, and the other two push, one person on each handle. For added fun, put blindfolds on the pushers and have the rider shout directions to the goal and back. It's fun to watch.

5. *Hand Wheelbarrow:* This is a wheelbarrow race minus a wheelbarrow. Two kids from each team compete. One kid lies face-down; the other grabs his feet like a wheelbarrow. The person on the ground walks on his hands; the person holding his feet holds him up and pushes.

6. *Wheelbarrow Hop:* In this relay, two members from each team compete at once. Place the wheelbarrow at the starting line with the handles facing forward (away from the team). The first pair stands on each side of the wheelbarrow, facing the same direction as the wheelbarrow. At a signal, they place their legs closest to the wheelbarrow into it in a kneeling position, grasp the handles in front of them, and hop to the marker and back. Penalties are given if anything but the wheel or the player's feet touch the ground.

CHAPTER TWO

Scavenger Hunts

Remember your first scavenger hunt? Chances are you do. You and your friends were given a list of ordinary things to find—a theater ticket, an empty Coca-Cola bottle, an old *T.V. Guide,* and a burned-out light bulb. You had about forty-five minutes to collect as many of these items as you could from houses in the neighborhood. Whichever group of kids came back with the most stuff won the game. Even though you felt a little foolish asking people if they had an old worn-out sock they could spare or a white jelly bean with red spots, you loved every minute of it.

Scavenger hunts have been popular with young people for many years. They are fun, competitive, and always an adventure; however, even a scavenger hunt can become boring if it's used too often. While all the activities in this chapter can be classified as scavenger hunts, each one is different and unique, giving a fresh new twist to a great old idea.

To make any scavenger hunt a success, advertise it well, create a carnival atmosphere, and plan a party afterward. To add to the fun, award crazy prizes for the winners and provide plenty of refreshments.

The rules for a scavenger hunt are simple. To begin, divide your group into teams of whatever size is appropriate. Give each team an identical list of items to bring back within a given time limit. The team bringing back the most is the winner. All of the ideas in this chapter fit that basic framework with some unusual variations.

★ A.B.C. SCAVENGER HUNT

Here's one that adds the element of chance to a scavenger hunt. Rather than creating a list of scavenger hunt items ahead of time, prepare several slips of paper with a letter of the *alphabet* written on each, preferably frequently-used consonants, such as "T," "S," "C," and "R." There should be one letter per team.

Each team draws one letter from a hat. If a team draws the "G," they must bring back only items that begin with the letter "G." For example, a "P" team might bring back a pot, a pickle, a peanut, and a Ping-Pong ball.

Set a time limit and have a scale handy. When the teams return, award bonus points for various types of items: Living things get twenty-five extra points, such as an animal, a plant, a person; anything weighing over twenty-five pounds gets forty extra points; anything edible gets ten extra points.

Other rules might include these: All items must be obtained for free (no purchases) and with the owner's permission (if the item has an owner). No items may be retrieved from a team member's home or car.

ACTION SCAVENGER HUNT

This is a scavenger hunt for *actions*, not objects. Give each team a list of actions. They are to find people, one per household, who will perform the designated action. Here's a sample list.

1. Sing two verses of "Old MacDonald Had a Farm."

2. Do ten jumping jacks.

3. Recite John 3:16.

4. Name five movies currently playing in local theaters.

5. Yodel something.

6. Run around your house.

7. Start your car's engine and honk the horn.

8. Take our picture with *your* camera.

9. Whistle one verse of "Yankee Doodle."
10. Say the Pledge of Allegiance.
11. Give us a guided tour of your garage.
12. Autograph the bottoms of our feet.
13. Say "bad blood" ten times really fast.
14. Belch.
15. Do a somersault.

Whenever a person performs one of the items on the list, he signs his name under that item to verify he did it. The team with the most signed-off items within the time limit is the winner.

★ AMOEBA SCAVENGER HUNT

This idea can be combined with many of the others in this chapter to make your next scavenger hunt even more exciting or difficult. Team *agreement* is the key to completing this hunt successfully.

Link the team together, either inside a hula hoop or by safely tying them, so the team moves together as they travel. It's funny as well as frustrating when the team members want to go in several different directions at once.

AUTOGRAPH SCAVENGER HUNT

This is a scavenger hunt for *signatures*. Each item requires someone's signature, along with a phrase he must write. The teams must find the specified person and persuade him to write the phrase and sign it. Here are some examples.

1. A See's Candy store employee: "Sugar rots your teeth!"
2. A truck driver: "I hate country music!"
3. A kid under eight years of age: "I'm a spoiled brat!"
4. A minister: "Organ music makes me sick!"
5. Someone over sixty-five years of age: "I really dig rock and roll!"
6. A Chevrolet salesman: "Ford has a better idea!"

★ AUTO-GRAPH SCAVENGER HUNT

Give each team a stack of white letter-sized sheets of paper and a list, like the sample one, which includes a variety of cars and other *vehicles*. The team must get each vehicle's autograph—the imprint of the tire tread on the white paper. Points can be awarded depending on the difficulty of the vehicles on the list or specific vehicles, such as cars owned by members of the congregation. Ask a neutral judge or sponsor to travel with each group to verify the authenticity of the Auto-graphs.

1. A 1957 Chevy
2. Any car with the numbers "4," "5," and "6" in the license number
3. A church bus
4. A blue Ford
5. An ambulance
6. A Honda motorcycle
7. Any car with less than 500 miles on the odometer
8. A lawn mower
9. A fire truck
10. A ten-speed bike

11. Any car that has just driven over the 12th Street bridge

 CHURCH TRIVIA HUNT

This would be a good scavenger hunt to do as part of a LOCK-IN (an overnighter at the church). The teams or individuals need to bring back *information about the church* specified by the scavenger-hunt list. Divide and conquer is a good strategy for the teams. The first team to bring back all the information is the winner. Prepare a list of twenty or thirty items, similar to this sample list.

1. What company manufactured the fire extinguisher in the hallway?

2. How many steps lead into the baptistry?

3. How many fuses are in the fuse box?

4. Where is the church's first-aid kit?

5. What is the last word in the book *Mere Christianity* by C. S. Lewis?

6. How many yellow lines are painted on the church parking lot?

 COLLEGE SURVIVAL KIT SCAVENGER HUNT

This scavenger hunt combines fun with service. If your church has a number of young people who have gone to college, this scavenger hunt is designed to remember them in a special way. Divide into teams, one for each of the *collegians* you want to include. Give the teams a list, similar to the one below, that contains items to be sent to all the collegians you are remembering. After the hunt, each team can box their items, including written notes of explanation (the items will need some explanation), encouragement, and friendship. Here's a suggested list.

1. Cookies—any kind. Each team must get three dozen cookies, no more than six at any one house.

2. A coupon good for a discount at any fast-food restaurant (*very* valuable to a college student).

3. Two tea bags (for mellow evenings).

4. Two toothpicks (to hold their eyelids open during final-exam studying).

5. One package of instant soup (for those with rushed lunches or who tire of cafeteria food).

6. Hot chocolate (to drink while they are thinking of home).

7. Kleenex tissues (in case they get all choked up going through this box).

8. A flashlight battery (for burning the midnight oil).

9. A stamp (so they can write us a letter).

10. A church bulletin (so they'll know we are still here).

11. A quarter (so they can call someone if they get lonely).

★ **COMPARISON SCAVENGER HUNT**

In this scavenger hunt, rather than bringing back specific items, the teams bring back the oldest, the ugliest, or the biggest *in comparison to what the other teams find.* After all the teams return from the hunt, read the list, one item at a time, and ask each team to display their entry for that particular item. On items that are somewhat subjective, such as the ugliest or smelliest, have a panel of experts determine the winner. The team with the most winning entries wins the event. Here's a sample list.

1. The biggest book

2. The oldest nickel

3. The smelliest sock

4. The most worn-out shoe

5. The ugliest picture

6. The longest stick

7. The funniest cartoon

8. The rustiest tin can

9. An advertisement for the most expensive car

★ CRAZY-CREATIVE SCAVENGER HUNT

As its name implies, this activity is *crazy* and requires a lot of *creative thinking*, but lots of fun. Here's how it works: Give your scavenger-hunt teams a list of items that don't make any sense. They are either nonsense words or items that don't seem to exist, such as this sample list.

1. A Zipper Zapper
2. Chicken Lips
3. A Yellow Grot Grabber
4. A Galvanized Ghoul Gooser
5. A Thumb Twiddly Dummer

6. A Thingamabob
7. An Idaho-de-ho
8. A P. B. J.
9. A Pine Needle Bushing Brush
10. A Snail Egg

The teams must find items that best fit the names, words, or phrases on this list and a good reason why theirs is the genuine article. For example, if they bring their Thumb Twiddly Dummer, then they must state why theirs is the *true* Thumb Twiddly Dummer because other teams will have a different item that they claim is a Thumb Twiddly Dummer. Which is the correct one? A panel of judges can decide. You'll be amazed at what your kids will bring back.

 DATE SCAVENGER HUNT
Divide into teams and give each one a list of *years* (1986, 1985, 1984) from the present year working backward for about thirty years or so. The kids need to collect items that have those years indelibly marked on them. They can bring back license plates, coins, drivers licenses, books with copyright dates, deeds, certificates, or old magazines.

This scavenger hunt has one important rule to encourage creativity—only one item per date is allowed. For instance, if the team brings back a *book* for the date 1965, then they cannot use a book for any other date.

 FUNGI HUNT
This is probably the *zaniest* scavenger hunt in this chapter. If your group likes things that are really out of the ordinary and has the courage to do some rather outrageous things, they will enjoy this hunt. In some ways, this special event is a combination of the ACTION SCAVENGER HUNT (p. 56) and the THE GREAT RACE (p. 64).

Divide into carloads and send the kids out with a list of instructions. Like any other scavenger hunt, the object is to fulfill the requirements of as many items on the list as possible within the specified time limit; however, no two items on the list can be finished at the same place. The driver of the car, or any adult accompanying each team, can verify that items checked off the list were properly completed. Here's a sample list.

1. Go to a donut shop and buy a donut of your choice. The donut must be brought back to the church with a bite taken out of it by the person who sold the donut to you.

2. Get the entire group to go to a Big Boy restaurant and point at the top of the "Big Boy" (statue) for two minutes.

3. Get thirty marshmallows from a single block of homes, no more than five marshmallows allowed per house.

4. Get the whole group to sit in a tree for one minute.

5. Go to someone's home who is in your group. File quietly into the house and sit down at the kitchen table. In unison ask, "What's for dinner, Mom?" As soon as the mother comes out of shock, you may file out.

6. Go to a Baskin-Robbins Ice Cream Store. Have one person order a milk shake *without any ice cream in it*.

7. At a fairly long traffic signal, everyone gets out of the car, runs around it once, then gets back in before the light turns green.

8. Go to a grocery store and have each member of the group ask the same salesperson (checker) where to find a box of prunes. Space yourselves, so he doesn't know you are all together. Be as polite as possible.

9. Go to the house of one of the people in your group. Everyone file into the bathroom, shut the door, flush the toilet, and then file back out.

10. Go to a McDonald's restaurant. Go inside, and everyone gets down on his hands and knees and pretends he's looking for someone's lost contact lens for about three minutes.

11. Go to a restaurant and have everyone gather around the waitress of your choice and sing, "For she's a jolly good waitress!"

12. In your car, go to the house of someone whose father is probably home. When you get there, each person should shake hands with that father, saying, "Sure is good to see you, sir!"

13. Can you stuff everyone in your car into a phone booth? Try.

14. Go to a shopping mall and ask a tall, bald man what time it is.

15. Go to a gas station and seriously ask directions to the place right across the street from that particular gas station.

16. Walk through the Broadway Department Store, holding hands, and with one person in your group wearing swim fins.

17. Go stand in front of city hall, face the flag, and sing the national anthem.

18. Go to a grocery store, buy one orange, and have the checkout person autograph it for you.

★ **THE GREAT RACE**

The Great Race is a scavenger hunt for *information*, usually best completed in cars, although it can be done on bikes or even on foot. Appoint drivers who are responsible and will obey all traffic laws. Each carload (team) is given a list, similar to the one below.

As youth leaders, you will need to compile a good list of about twenty-five items from around town. Some can be easy to find; others can be difficult. Provide each team with a map of the area and possibly a telephone book, so they can look up the location of places they aren't familiar with. Since the list requires information from all over town, advise teams to map out a route or strategy before they hit the road. Items on the list can be taken in any order. The team returning with the most correct information within the specified time limit is the winner.

1. Who made the light pole on the corner of Main and Broadway?

2. What color is the sign at Jerry's Dog Grooming?

3. What event is advertised on the poster hanging over the water fountain inside the Lakeside Safeway Store?

4. How much is the total cost (including tax) of the following items at the Cotija Taco Shop?

> Two beef tacos, three cheese enchiladas, one carne asada burrito, five rolled tacos with guacamole, ten tamales, and three medium Diet Cokes.

5. Who donated the gum-ball machine at Wally's Texaco?

6. When was Pinecrest School founded? By whom?

7. How many lights are blinking on the KSON Radio Tower?

8. What kind of flowers are blooming in front of the Harold Farnsworthy home on Madison Street?

 THE GREAT RACE #2

Here's another way to do The Great Race, which makes it a little more challenging. Rather than giving teams all the questions on the list, give them only one (each team gets a different one) and some coins. When they have the correct answer to that question, they must find a phone booth and call Great Race Central to get another question. The teams are forced to answer the questions in a given order and they never know what is coming next.

 INTELLECTUAL SCAVENGER HUNT

Here's a scavenger for all the eggheads in the group. They must figure out *what the list means* before they know what to bring back. Use a thesaurus to create a list, similar to the one below, using the biggest words you can find.

1. A cylindrical object that releases a blue medium used to communicate (a pen that writes in blue ink).

2. A many-pronged black object used by the vain (a black comb).

3. When exhaled into, this highly elastic substance expands and enlarges into a flimsy, spherical object (a round balloon).

4. The product of a fructiferous vegetation, ocher in color and quite elongated (a banana).

5. An intricately engraved document with a verdant hue used to procure commodities from retail emporiums (a dollar bill).

6. A sanitary, pliant piece of fabric used to swab mucus from one's nasal cavities (a handkerchief).

★ **INTERVIEW SCAVENGER HUNT**

This scavenger hunt is not only a lot of fun but can also be very educational. Busy places, such as a shopping mall, an airport, or an amusement park provide the best locations for this activity. The scavenger-hunt list contains a *list of questions* that the kids must ask a variety of people. The questions can be serious or off-the-wall.

Instruct your kids to treat each person whom they interview with respect, to listen to him, and to write down as accurately as possible his answer—only one person per question allowed. If anyone refuses to be interviewed, don't bother him further. When the kids return, read the questions one-by-one and have kids share the responses they received. Whichever team has the most answers within the given time limit wins. Here's a sample list.

1. Ask someone to describe his most embarrassing moment.

2. Ask someone to give his opinion of the president's foreign policy.

3. Ask a taxicab driver to describe the most interesting person he has ever had as a customer.

4. Ask any person who is working why he chose his particular occupation.

5. Ask a child under ten years of age to describe God.

6. Find a policeman and ask him, "If you could give a teenager one bit of advice, what would it be?"

7. Ask someone to describe the best vacation he ever had.

★ **MISSION IMPOSSIBLE**

For this scavenger hunt, teams are given a list of *Impossible Missions* that they must try to accomplish within the given time limit. There is one important rule—teams may *not* tell anyone why they are doing what they are doing until after the mission has been accomplished. The team to accomplish successfully the most missions is the winner. Here are some samples.

1. Get a signed statement from a doctor that no one in your group has the bubonic plague.

2. Talk a taxi driver into driving your group around the block for only one dollar.

3. Get an airline pilot to show you the inside of a 747's cockpit.

4. Go to a radio station and try to get "on the air."

5. Go to a city council member and complain that the city is not doing enough to help teenagers find summer jobs.

6. Do a rain dance for five minutes around the fountain in the city park.

7. See if you can "buy a kiss" from someone.

8. Persuade a minister to perform a funeral for your dear departed pet turtle.

 MYSTERY SCAVENGER HUNT

In this scavenger hunt, kids get a list of *clues* to solve before they know what to bring back. Instruct the kids to decipher the clues in any order they wish. If they can't figure out a clue, they can call a special phone number to get the answer; however, they receive half the point value if the item is found. Here's a sample clue list with the answers in parentheses.

Section One: House-to-House (One Point Each)

You must figure out the item clue and go to the homes of persons who are *not* in your church. Tell them what you are doing and ask them if they have the item and would give it to you.

1. A small object mentioned in the lyrics of Petra's song "Judas Kiss." (nail)

2. Mug Foe Cei Pa. (a piece of gum)

3. This comes runny, but bring in a hard one. (hard-boiled egg)

4. Fish hate these. (hook)

5. This explodes, but it's not made of metal. (firecracker)

6. This is listed in the phone book on page 74 of the yellow pages, four inches from the left side of the page and three inches from the top. (salt)

7. This works well for getting liquid out of paper receptacles. (straw)

Section Two: Places Around Town (Two Points Each)
You must figure out the place clue and go there to buy the item as soon as you figure out the item clue. You must bring back a receipt or some sort of proof that you bought it at the right place.

1. *Place:* Market where Smokey shops. (Big Bear) *Item:* It is usually sold in groups; it's not grown in the North; it must be at least seven inches long. (banana)

2. *Place:* The hardiest place in town. (Hardee's) *Item:* Spend between you fifty-seven cents for something that's not sweet (hamburger).

3. *Place:* Sandcastles help ostriches pay kings' offerings. (Shopko store—S.H.O.P.K.O.) *Item:* A candy bar advertised with Elvis in its T.V. commercial. (Hershey Bar)

4. *Place:* ///////// - ////////////. (7-11) *Item:* This comes in a bottle, but most of us drink it from cans. It's not old or new, but it's kind of like both. George Washington wouldn't have liked it; neither would a person who is trying to gain weight. It won't make you nervous. (Diet Caffeine-free Coke)

Section Three: Anywhere You Can Find 'Em (One Point Each)
1. This is what they give you when you pay to see what they are showing. (movie ticket stub)

2. This is white, hard in the middle, and soft at the ends. (Q-tip)

3. Don't take this off of your car or else you won't get back to the church. We want an old worn-out one. (tire)

4. People are hitting these right in stadiums. (baseballs)

5. This one is flat and black with a hole, which celebrates the birthday of someone who is very important. (Christmas record)

6. This foul item might just tickle you. (feather)

7. This is a dollar bill. Isn't that easy? But we want one with three 7's in the serial number.

PEOPLE SCAVENGER HUNT

This activity can also be called a Manhunt. Give each team a list of *people* (not specific names) whom they have to find and persuade to *voluntarily* join their group for the rest of the hunt. Obviously, if the team is successful, their group will grow in size as the evening progresses. At the conclusion of the hunt, plan a party honoring all the guests and award team points for the people, according to difficulty in finding them. A sample list follows:

1. A varsity football player
2. A student-body officer
3. Someone who can speak Spanish
4. Someone who weighs more than two hundred pounds
5. A cheerleader
6. Someone who plays a tuba
7. A girl with red hair
8. Someone with more than ten letters in his last name
9. Someone over six feet tall
10. Someone who drives a motorcycle

 POLAROID SCAVENGER HUNT

Here's one that your group will want to do again and again. Give each team an instant camera (one that develops its own photos), a couple rolls of film, and a list of pictures to take. If this event is in the evening, they will also need some flashbulbs or a flash attachment. Each picture is worth a certain number of points—the more difficult the picture, the more points. Some sample pictures are included here.

Get a picture of your entire group:

1. Hanging by their knees from a tree limb (10 pts.).
2. Climbing a flagpole with the bottom person at least three feet off the ground (15 pts.).
3. Inside a police car (25 pts.) with the policeman (35 pts.).

4. Next to an airplane (40 pts.), inside the airplane (75 pts.), and inside the cockpit (100 pts.) with the pilot and a stewardess (125 pts.).

5. Next to a tombstone in a cemetery (10 pts.).

6. Next to a clock tower that reads exactly 6:22 P.M. (50 pts.).

7. In someone's (a stranger's) bathtub (40 pts.).

8. Making French fries at a McDonald's restaurant (35 pts.).

9. On a roof (20 pts.).

10. Inside a telephone booth (10 pts.) with two other people who are not part of your group (30 pts.).

11. In a boat on water (25 pts.).

12. Dressed in Halloween costumes, trick or treating at someone's house (50 pts.).

13. Standing in front of the mayor's house (15 pts.) with the major (60 pts.).

Your list should include plenty of possibilities for photos—some easy ones and plenty of difficult ones. You'll be surprised at what your kids will do. Each team should have a chaperon or driver who also takes the pictures. Each picture must have every person on the team in it, unless specified otherwise. For pictures that have more than one option (for example, #4 in the above list), only one may be taken.

At the end of the time limit, the teams return to the meeting place and display all their pictures. Points are tallied, and prizes awarded to the winners. Usually, each team will have good stories to tell about their experiences that evening. The pictures can be saved and put in your youth group's scrapbook or annual.

A slight variation of the Polaroid Scavenger Hunt is another event called Polaroid Portraits, combining the POLAROID SCAVENGER HUNT with the PEOPLE SCAVENGER HUNT (p. 70). Give each team a list of people to photograph, all of whom are not a part of the group (complete strangers, if possible). Again, assign photos a point value, according to their difficulty. Here's a suggested list.

1. Someone wearing a L.A. Dodgers baseball cap

2. A child with a balloon

3. A pair of twins

4. Someone asleep on a park bench

5. Two people kissing each other

6. A policeman arresting someone

7. Someone showing hostility and anger

8. A clown

9. Someone with a punk hairdo

10. A serviceman in uniform

 RAINBOW SCAVENGER HUNT

This is a scavenger hunt for *colors.* Go to your local paint store and pick up a few paint color charts. Then, give each team one of those charts. The teams must find items that match the colors on the chart—any item will do, but it has to match *exactly.* Judges can disqualify any item that is questionable. Extra points are given for items that have only the matched color on it, the *most* of the matched color, and the least of the matched color. Paint and art stores are off-limits.

★ **SAFARI SCAVENGER HUNT**

Next time your group visits an *amusement park or tourist attraction,* combine it with a scavenger hunt that lasts the entire day. Safari Scavenger Hunt is designed for a trip to the local zoo. After your group arrives at the zoo, divide into small groups of three or four who stay together during the day and give each group a list of things to do and things to find. At the end of the day, award prizes (or souvenirs) to the groups that complete the most items on the list. A sample list for the zoo is included.

1. Make up a song about your youth pastor, an elephant, and a monkey.

2. Bring back some animal food.

3. Who is "Sam"? (The name of an animal in the zoo.)

4. Get the signature of a female animal trainer.

5. Which is the youngest animal in the zoo?

6. What is an "Oxyrinchus Picanosis?"

7. Find the "Australian Grodfog" and describe it here: (a lady you have sitting on a bench near the kangaroos, dressed strangely and wearing a fake mustache).

8. Talk to a monkey for five minutes without stopping and have a complete stranger sign here to verify that you did it.

9. Ask a child if you can taste his cotton candy. Stick some of it here:

10. Which animal mates only once every three years?

11. Volunteer to take a picture of a group of Japanese tourists. Have one of them sign here.

12. Get someone in a wheelchair to run over this piece of paper and sign it.

 ST. PATRICK'S DAY SCAVENGER HUNT

Here's a good scavenger hunt for St. Patty's Day. Have the kids look for *green things.* Either you can provide a long list of green items for them to pick from, or you can just let them bring back as many green things as they can within the given time limit. They cannot bring back two things alike (two green shirts) and are not allowed to pick any green plants, except a shamrock (four-leaf clover), which is worth extra points.

 SCAVENGER HUNT SWITCH

Here's a great scavenger hunt idea that will really take your group by *surprise.* To begin, divide the group into smaller scavenger hunt teams. Then, tell each team to write down ten of the hardest items (within reason) they can think of for a scavenger hunt to be given to another team. Stress that they should not put anything on the list that would be impossible to find, but give the other team a good, challenging hunt.

After each team has compiled their list of ten items, have them exchange lists with one other team. Allow them some time to moan and complain about their new list, then tell each team to switch back to their original list because they actually have to find the items on their own list.

SCRIPTURE SCAVENGER HUNT

Here's one that combines fun with some Bible learning. Teams try to bring back *items that can be found in the Bible.* For example, they might bring back a stick (Moses' rod), or a rock (the stoning of Stephen), or a loaf of bread (the Last Supper). Every item must be accompanied by a Bible verse to prove that it can be found in the Bible. The team to return with the most items is the winner.

 SCRIPTURE SCAVENGER HUNT #2

As a variation, give teams a list of specific verses that contain items to be brought back, like the ones below. You might want to agree upon which version is to be used.

1. Luke 15:8—A woman had ten of something. You bring in the same. (ten silver coins)

2. Matthew 16:19—Jesus said he would give Peter something. Bring one back. (a key)

3. Revelation 11:1—Bring in something we use today like what John was given. (a measuring instrument)

4. Mark 14:20—Jesus dipped bread into something. Bring one in. (a dish)

5. Isaiah 24:13—Bring back one of the two things you could eat. (an olive or a grape)

6. Matthew 5:13—Bring in what Jesus says we are. (salt)

7. I Peter 2:2—Bring in some of the drink found here. (milk)

8. Hebrews 1:9—God has anointed thee with the _____ of gladness. Bring any kind. (oil)

9. Luke 15:17—Bring in what the servants have plenty of. (bread)

10. James 1:11—Something falls off. Bring one in. (flower)

SERVICE SCAVENGER HUNT

Throw tradition into reverse with this scavenger hunt. Instead of collecting a list of items, *give* a list of items. Each team of scavengers is given a list of service projects to do within a specified time limit. The list can include items like these:

1. Mow someone's lawn.
2. Sweep three driveways.
3. Wash the windows in someone's home.
4. Wash someone's car.
5. Vacuum the carpets in someone's home.
6. Wash someone's dishes.
7. Remove all the weeds from someone's lawn or garden.
8. Sing a few songs to a senior citizen shut-in.

Anything on this list should be something that can be accomplished quickly and easily by most kids. The kids must understand that the important thing is doing a good job at each location and giving themselves unselfishly. They need to ask permission to do all the things they do and cannot accept money for what they do. Courtesy and carefulness for others' property are the rules to remember. Allow the groups to repeat items for extra points, for example, they can mow *three* lawns or wash *two* cars. At the end of the hunt, ask the kids to share their experiences with each other. The kids will feel good about what they have done; so will the neighborhood.

 SERVICE SCAVENGER HUNT #2

Here's another way to combine a scavenger hunt with a *service* project. Give kids a list of items that when collected, can be given to the local rescue mission, missionaries overseas, or to a needy family in the community. The list can include canned goods, new or used clothing, shoes, or household items. Kids try to collect as much as possible within the given time limit. If the kids tell people what they are doing, they will have a lot of success. You, as well as they, will be amazed at how much they bring back when they not only compete against each other but also work for a worthy cause.

★ **SHOPPING-MALL DERBY**

Plan this activity in a large *shopping mall*, although it is also possible in any downtown or suburban shopping area. It's similar to THE GREAT RACE (p. 64), only without cars. Have all the kids meet at a central location and then pair off or form small groups of three or four. Give each group a list, like the sample one, and pencils. They have an hour to find the answers to each item on the list. The team with the most correct answers is the winner. If there is a fast-food restaurant in the mall, meet there for refreshments afterward and award prizes (free ice cream sundaes?).

A word of caution: It may be necessary to clear this event with the shopping mall management ahead of time, especially if a large group of kids is involved. This event has the potential to be disruptive to shoppers and merchants unless precautions are taken. Make sure your kids understand they are not to be rude, loud, or disruptive during the event. No running is allowed, and if it is necessary to talk to a store clerk, they must wait in line, if necessary, and be polite, always thanking people for their help.

Obviously, you will need to go to the shopping mall ahead of time to prepare your list, about twenty-five questions. List only items that will be there when your group goes. Usually, it is best to prepare your list no earlier than the day before your event (or even earlier the same day). Here's a sample list.

1. What store is using a Hawaiian theme to sell clothing?

2. What is the number on the "Think Snow" sticker at Sunshine Shirts?

3. What is the maximum occupancy of the Family Fun Center?

4. How many mirrors hang from the ceiling at T.G. & Y.?

5. What is the price of a "Great Patagonian Conure" and where is it sold?

6. What store has an inflatable zeppelin hanging near the door?

7. Who plays drums on the record album "Where Rainbows Touch Down" by the Bluegrass Cardinals?

8. What merchandise is on page 1124 of the Sears catalog?

9. What is the "flavor of the month" at Baskin-Robbins?

10. In what store is a mannequin wearing a football helmet?

11. What is the #8 best-selling paperback book at B. Dalton?

12. In what store can you buy a TX-135 direct-drive turntable?

13. How many pairs of shoes are in the store window at Kirby's Shoes?

14. What is the single most expensive item on display and for sale in the entire shopping mall? (The team finding the most expensive item wins.)

★ **SHOPSCOTCH**

Plan this hunt for a *shopping mall* or a shopping area where there are plenty of stores. Give each team an envelope with two dollars in cash and a list of items they must purchase with the money. The team with the most items and the most money left within the time limit is the winner. Receipts must be brought back with everything, including items obtained for free. Of course, shoplifting is a no-no. Visit the shopping area ahead of time to make certain the items on the list are obtainable. The following is a sample list.

1. One paint card sample

2. Pocket-sized Kleenex

3. An empty pop bottle

4. Any toy

5. Six peanuts in the shell
6. A piece of fruit
7. A pea shooter
8. A travel brochure to anywhere
9. Twelve inches of ribbon
10. Toothpaste squeeze keys
11. Apple Blossom soap
12. A piece of candy
13. A noisemaker
14. One slice of pizza
15. Anything purchased from a jewelry store

★ SOUND SCAVENGER HUNT

This one is like the POLAROID SCAVENGER HUNT (p. 70), only *cassette tape recorders* instead of instant cameras are used. Provide each team with a tape recorder, a blank cassette tape, and a list of sounds, like those below, that they have to record.

1. A dog barking
2. A siren from a police car, ambulance, fire engine
3. Somebody playing a tune on a violin
4. A cash register opening and closing
5. A crying baby
6. Someone doing an impression of James Cagney
7. Tire screeching on the pavement
8. Someone over sixty-five years of age explaining what the word "macho" means
9. A toilet flushing
10. Someone singing opera

★ TOMBSTONE SCAVENGER HUNT

As the name implies, a *cemetery* is the best setting for this hunt, especially around Halloween. Unless you are using an old deserted cemetery, ask permission first and notify the police and the neighbors about what's happening. Make a list of names found on tombstones and have the kids try to locate them and write in the dates found on the tombstone for that person.

VIDEO SCAVENGER HUNT
Do POLAROID SCAVENGER HUNT (p. 70) with video cameras.

 WILDERNESS SCAVENGER HUNT
Here's a scavenger hunt list that might come in handy when your group is *outdoors* near a river or a lake, in the woods, at a park, or at a camp or retreat.

the words of John 15:13
a piece of flint rock
a flea
a yellow wild flower
a pre-1975 penny
a snail
a three-inch twig
a four-leaf clover
a string of ten pop tops
a paper clip
a pine needle
five different soda caps
a feather
a mosquito
an acorn
a root-beer can
an old, colored sock
a piece of rope
a baby diaper
a golf tee
a snuff can
a match box
a toothpick
a little live fishie
a double pine cone
a piece of hard, used gum

a cotton ball
a corncob
a Salem cigarette
a dandelion
a magazine
a brick
a cactus needle
a mesquite bean pod
a live fly
a mushroom
a piece of ribbon
a button
a clean Kleenex
a red leaf
a piece of green glass
a strip of cassette tape
a red handkerchief
a pencil that isn't yellow
a new piece of charcoal
a rubber band
a walking stick
an out-of-town newspaper
a crayon
some moss
a mud dauber's home
a plastic 6-pack holder

a live grasshopper
a ticket stub
an apple core
three live ants
a red shoestring
a lizard
a cigar band

a straw
a Popsicle stick
a roly-poly bug
a used stamp
a live frog
a bun with sesame seeds
a 1979 calendar

★ CHAPTER THREE ★

Treasure Hunts

The treasure hunt is another old stand-by and one of the best activities for youth. This chapter is a guide to enable you to inject new life into this old idea and make it an exciting experience every time you do it.

Most treasure hunts are essentially the same. Like a scavenger hunt, there are teams or small groups that try to find the treasure by following a series of clues. One clue leads to another clue, until finally the last clue leads to the treasure. The first team to bring back the treasure is the winner.

There are many ways to make every treasure hunt unique. By changing the treasure, by changing the type of clues, or by changing the mode of transportation, you can use the basic structure of a treasure hunt and create variations.

★ THE TREASURE

First, when you rename the event, you make a new event. The name that you choose can be determined by the treasure. Here are a few examples.

1. *A Great Pumpkin Hunt:* The treasure is a giant pumpkin, ideal for Halloween.

2. *Witch Hunt:* Perfect for Halloween—hide a witch, made from old clothing filled with straw. After the witch is found, burn it at the stake.

3. *A Giant Easter Egg Hunt:* Make a giant decorated egg out of chicken wire and papier mâché.

4. *A Wild Goose Chase:* Hide a live goose and have teams try to bring it back alive!

5. *Search for the Abominable Snowman:* The youth sponsors build an Abominable Snowman. The hunters travel either on foot, on cross-country skis, or on snowmobiles.

6. *Submarine Races:* The treasure is a toy model submarine, which, when found, must be put together. The first team to finish the model with the decals, too, is the winner. Serve submarine sandwiches for refreshments.

7. *Raiders of the Lost Ark:* Build the ark of the covenant for this treasure. Have kids wear Indiana Jones outfits and show the popular movie afterward.

The possibilities are endless, so create your own treasure hunts by making the treasure something novel.

★ **THE HUNT BEGINS**
Have everyone meet at a certain time and place, then assign them into groups to travel together. Most treasure hunts are done in cars,

although any mode of transportation can be used. Some large groups of more than one thousand young people have actually done treasure hunts using a fleet of busses. If your hunt is conducted in a confined area, teams can travel on foot or perhaps use bicycles. If you do use cars, be certain your drivers are mature and have insurance as well as a driver's license.

Before the hunt begins, gather everyone together to explain the rules. If your groups are large, have each group appoint a leader or captain and explain the rules only to them; they can explain the rules to their teams.

The rules should include the following:

1. *The Time Limit:* At a certain time, the hunt is over, regardless of whether the treasure has been found. Your time limit should be determined ahead of time, depending on the number of clues and their difficulty.

2. *Explanation of the Clue Packet:* Each team will receive a clue packet, which contains certain items that may or may not be essential to solving the clues.

3. *Safety Precautions:* If kids are traveling by car, make sure they obey all traffic laws and don't interfere with the driver's responsibility, which is to drive the car. Seat belts should be worn at all times. Any other safety precautions should also be discussed.

After the rules are explained, the first clue is given to each team or team captain. The clue should be sealed in an envelope. After all have their first clue, the signal to begin is given, and the teams open the clue and try to solve it as quickly as possible. As soon as they figure out the first clue, they go to where that clue leads to find their second clue.

As a variation, rather than giving the team captains the first clue itself, give them a sheet of instructions like the one on the following page. They must follow the directions on the sheet before they get the first clue.

★ THE CLUES

Assign each team or vehicle a number. To prevent groups from simply following each other to the treasure, plan a different route for each group, so they all go to the same clue locations in a different order. Give each team about the same overall distance to travel.

Each clue will take the team to one of six locations, more or less depending on how long the hunt is and how difficult the clues are. The last location is the treasure's location. If a team cheats by locating the treasure without working out the solution to all the clues, they are penalized or disqualified. Find unusual clue locations, such as the top of a church tower, a boat in the middle of a lake, up in a tree, buried in a cemetery, in an airport terminal, or at a tourist attraction.

TO RECEIVE YOUR FIRST CLUE, COMPLETE THE INSTRUCTIONS BELOW

1. Please read all the directions on this sheet before doing anything else.

2. Total up the ages of everyone in your group. _____

3. List the middle names of everyone in your group. _____

4. Have someone in your group do ten push-ups.

5. Have your group yell three times as loud as they can, "We're Number One!"

6. Write one Bible verse of your choice here. _____
_____
_____

7. If you followed direction #1 and read all the directions first, then you do not have to do instructions #2–6. Mark an "X" in the upper right hand corner, turn in your sheet, get your first clue, and begin hunting. Good luck!

★ THE CLUE GIVERS

Ask a youth sponsor or another neutral adult to hand out the clues as the teams arrive at the clue location. Number the clues for each location to prevent confusion. To add to the fun, have the clue giver hidden at the clue location, so the hunters have to look around a little bit to find him. For example, if the clue location is a restaurant, the clue giver could be inside the restaurant, sitting at a table. Remember to get permission from the manager or owner if you use a store, restaurant, or other business establishment for clue locations.

Here's another variation—use clue givers who are strangers to the kids in the group. Then, have the kids find each clue giver by using a secret word or phrase, which they must say to the clue giver at each location. For example, if you are doing a Wild Goose Chase, the kids say, "Goosey Goosey Gander, Where Do You Wander?" to everyone they see at the clue location until they find the clue giver. If you use clue locations where there are lots of people, like a department store, a tourist attraction, or a busy street corner, it's hilarious.

★ CREATING THE CLUES

Next to the treasure itself, the clues are the most important part of the treasure hunt. Make them fun, yet challenging. Your treasure hunt will be most exciting if you use a variety of clues, not the same type of clue at each clue location. Don't underestimate your kids' clue-solving ability. Here are a few clue ideas.

1. Inside the envelope are several letters from a Scrabble game. (To solve this clue, the letters must be put in their correct order to spell out the name of the location.)

2. Inside the envelope is a piece of adding machine tape with a list of numbers. (To solve this clue, the team must add up the numbers, the sum of which is a telephone number to call for the next clue location.)

3. The clue can be a "rebus," which you create. On the next page are some samples.

4. The clue can be a difficult-to-recognize photograph of the location. For example, the photo might be of a boat, and the kids must find that particular boat at the local harbor.

5. The clue might be something like this:

```
H.F., page 136.
```

under office stairs

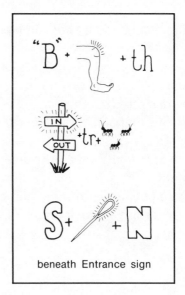

beneath Entrance sign

(To solve this clue, the group decides this is a book and deciphers the book title [*Huckleberry Finn*], goes to the library, looks up page 136, and there they find the next clue location.)

6. A Bible verse or a series of Bible verses. (To solve this clue, the group reads the verse(s) to find the next clue location.

There are unlimited possibilities for clues. Don't worry that the group won't solve the clue because there will be emergency clues in the clue packet if they get stumped.

★ THE CLUE PACKETS

At the beginning of the treasure hunt, give each group a manila envelope full of things that may or may not be important to them. Tell each team to familiarize themselves with the contents of the packet immediately. Here are some suggestions for things to include in the clue packet.

1. *The Hunt Map:* This is an ordinary road map. Mark the map with numbers and arrows pointing to a variety of locations. More locations are marked than there are clue locations, but *only* those locations marked on the map are possible clue locations.

2. *The Rules.*

3. *Helpful Hints:* Include this sheet with a random list of phrases that might help solve one of the clues. To create a little confusion, there should be more phrases than clues. Chances are they will come in handy if the group is stuck on a clue. For example, the list might include these items:

Sum Fun	(for the adding machine tape clue)
Silence, Please	(for the library)
Third	(the street the house is on)

4. *Miscellaneous Items:* Various odds and ends can be included, some of which might be useful. For example, a quarter can be included to make the phone call that one of the clues require.

5. *Emergency Clues:* If a group is unable to figure out a clue, then they can open an emergency clue, which is numbered and sealed just like the normal clues. Teams should open an emergency clue after they have worked without success on the regular clue for ten or fifteen minutes. However, when the groups arrive at the final clue location (the treasure), they must turn in all their emergency clues. For every opened emergency clue, they must wait a certain amount of time (ten to twenty minutes) before they can claim the treasure. If another group arrives while they are serving their penalty time, the other group can claim the treasure, if they have not opened any emergency clues.

A FEW REMINDERS

If the treasure is not found, the winner is determined by who got the farthest along the route using the least amount of emergency clues. This rarely happens if you plan enough time so everyone will get to the treasure within the time limit.

It is usually a good idea to have the last clue location be a place where your After-the-Hunt Party can be held. Serve refreshments, award prizes, and share experiences. If the treasure itself is not something that the hunters can keep, then have some appropriate prizes for the winning team and present the trophy to the team captain as dramatically and humorously as possible.

 TREASURE HUNT VARIATIONS

Here are a few other treasure-hunt ideas.

1. *House-to-House Puzzle Hunt:* In this treasure hunt, the teams pick up one puzzle piece of a large children's puzzle at each clue location. Whichever team completes the puzzle first wins.

2. *Caroling Treasure Hunt:* The teams (each with a different list of songs) sing a few Christmas carols at each clue location, such as a convalescent home, a shut-in's home, or the middle of a shopping mall. After the carols are sung, someone gives the group their next clue.

3. *Get-Acquainted Treasure Hunt:* The homes of church members provide the clue locations. When the group arrives at each home, they must go in and meet the members of that family and remain there for at least five minutes before they receive the next clue. During the five minutes, they should get acquainted with the people who live there.

4. *Memorization Treasure Hunt:* This one combines Bible memorization with a treasure hunt. At each location, there is a Bible verse posted that the group must memorize before they receive their next clue.

5. *Pirate Treasure Hunt:* Buried treasure and a treasure map are used for this hunt. Teams are given a treasure map of the city and a list of instructions, like those below.

1. From the NW corner of the quadrant marked Well-spring, draw a line to the center point of the northern edge of the map. From the SW corner of Central Park, draw a line to the southernmost point of Mapleview Road. Go to where these two lines intersect and find the telephone pole with the letters BN stamped on its eastern side.

2. From that location, proceed directly west along the picket fence for approximately 1000 yards. Face due north and look for two tall trees that line up with the water tower on the eastern slope of Johnson Hill. Go to the second of the two trees and stand under its lowest branch.

3. From that point, face the elephant and walk 40 paces. Turn left on a 90-degree angle and walk 40 more paces. Now turn right 90 degrees and walk 55 paces. Locate a large flat rock on the ground. Look under that rock.

Under the rock can be another set of instructions or the treasure itself.

6. *Progressive-Dinner Hunt:* This is simply a treasure hunt where each clue leads to the next course of a progressive dinner. Obviously, there is a lot of incentive for solving the clues!

★ CHAPTER FOUR ★

Car Rallies

Car rallies are in many ways similar to scavenger hunts and treasure hunts. Participants are divided into groups or teams that travel together around a predetermined course in cars or other vehicles. In most cases, the object is to be the first team to reach the final destination; in other cases, the object is to figure out the correct course, get the farthest away, or solve a puzzle.

As with any event that involves traveling by automobile, make sure that you have experienced, mature drivers who have good driving records and insurance and that everyone agrees to obey all speed and traffic laws. It's also a good idea to have all the participants contribute something to help pay for gas.

To prevent speeding, have a neutral adult sponsor ride in the back seat of each car. The sponsor has a dozen raw eggs. When the car is moving, the sponsor holds an egg on a spoon outside the window. If the car goes too fast, hits a bump too hard, or swerves too quickly, the egg will fall off and a new one must be put on the spoon. At the end of the car rally, the team that brings back the most unbroken eggs gets extra points or a bonus prize.

Here are some outstanding car rally ideas.

★ CLUE CAR RALLY
Based on the popular game Clue, the whole city is used for the game board. Although the rules look a bit complicated, they aren't difficult to understand.

A murder has been committed by one of ten suspects. It is known that the murderer used one of ten weapons and committed the crime in one of ten rooms in the victim's house on one of seven days of the week. It is also known that his motive for killing the victim was one of ten reasons (a total of 47 possibilities).

Each team, traveling around the city by car, will attempt to determine the suspect, the weapon, the motive, the room, and the day of the murder. To do this, they must use a process of elimination by asking the suspects simple yes or no questions and by accumulating clue-card quarters. When properly matched, four clue-card quarters will form an entire clue, which will eliminate one of the possibilities.

The suspects are located in houses or buildings all over the city, and the teams must travel to these locations as they question the suspects. The suspects can be adult sponsors, store employees, or complete strangers to the teams. There can be more than one suspect at each location.

Here's how the game is played.

Each team receives these items.
1. A clue sheet listing all the suspects, weapons, motives, rooms, and days to choose from. It is to be used as a worksheet as information is gathered.

2. A map showing the location of each suspect.

3. Four clue quarters that don't match to be given at the start of the game. Additional clue quarters are received at each location.

4. An accusation slip and an envelope. When a team is ready to make a final guess, the accusation slip is filled out, signed, sealed in the envelope, and handed to any of the suspects. The time to the second is recorded on the outside of the envelope when the suspect receives it. Once a team makes its guess, they are out of the game and return to headquarters, where there will be a party afterward.

Here's a clue sheet.

Suspects	Weapons	Motives	Rooms	Days
Maid	Knife	Money	Hall	Sunday
Milkman	Candlestick	Passion	Lounge	Monday
Playboy	Gun	Jealousy	Dining Room	Tuesday
Gardener	Rope	Power	Kitchen	Wednesday
Movie Star	Lead Pipe	Amusement	Ballroom	Thursday
Old Lady	Wrench	Accident	Closet	Friday
Farmer	Meat Cleaver	Greed	Library	Saturday
Butler	Hatchet	Hatred	Bathroom	
Singer	Poison	Fear	Parlor	
Magician	Shovel	Insanity	Garage	

Here's an accusation slip.

> The suspect who committed the crime was:
>
> The weapon used was a:
>
> The motive for the murder was:
>
> The room of the house was:
>
> The day of the week was:

Each team needs to decide a strategy for getting helpful information from each other along the way, if they think it might help their cause. The key is asking the right questions of the right suspects. Some questions will be lucky guesses; however, by determining who knows what, a team can be much more precise in its choice of questions.

Teams may ask each suspect privately two yes or no questions, such as "Was the murder weapon a knife?" Each of the ten suspects should be instructed to give information on only one of the five items involved in the crime. That means that two suspects will know who did it, two will know the weapon, and so on. If the suspect knows, he will answer yes or no; if he does not know, he will say, "I don't know." No team may question a suspect a second time until all the suspects have been questioned once. If more than one team arrives at a location simultaneously, then they may flip a coin to decide who gets to question the suspect first.

At each location, teams will receive a new clue-card quarter. When a matching set of clue-card quarters fits together, the finished clue will look something like this:

Butler 1	Butler 7
Butler 3	Butler 4

If the total of the four numbers on the clue is *even*, the answer is yes. If the total is *odd*, the answer is no. For example, the above clue would be no because the total is fifteen, so the butler is not a suspect. Clue-card quarters can be traded with other teams.

The winning team is the first to identify correctly each of the five parts of the mystery. A time limit should be set for all the teams to make a guess for the five parts to the mystery. At the Grand Opening of the

Accusations, the envelopes with the earliest time written on them are opened first. Award every team that guessed all five correctly a consolation prize.

★ CRAZY CAR RALLY

This car rally is very similar to some of the scavenger hunt ideas in chapter 2. Each team is given a route they must travel and a list of tasks they must perform along the way. The first team to finish the course and the tasks successfully is the winner.

Here's a sample route.

1. Go east on Main Street for seven blocks. Stop at the Union Bank building. Park on the fourth level of their parking lot (if full, wait until a space is available). Everyone get out of the car and go into the bank. One at a time, each member of your team must ride the elevator from the first floor to the twenty-first floor and back down. When finished, get back in your car and continue east on Main Street.

2. When you get to Dorsey Avenue, turn right. Stop at St. James Park. Everyone take the free tour of the science museum, which is every fifteen minutes. The tour lasts fifteen minutes. After you do this, get back in your car, turn right out of the parking lot, and continue west on Dorsey.

3. Turn left on Mapleview. Go to Mayor Smith's home, which is at 4352 Mapleview. Stand on the front lawn and sing any Christmas carol you wish.

4. Now, get on Highway 41 and head south. Use the trash bag provided and fill it full of litter from along the highway. Do not take any cans or trash from litter cans along the highway or pick up rocks, leaves, or wood. Do pick up only human trash, like paper, cans, bottles, or plastic.

Either give each team a different route and the same tasks, or start the cars at ten-minute intervals, recording the starting time for each car at the start and finish. Have a neutral adult sponsor ride with each team to insure that the tasks are properly done. The group that reaches the final destination in the shortest time is the winner.

★ CROSSWORD CAR RALLY

To win, the teams must complete a crossword puzzle. You will need to create your own puzzle. Give each team a printed copy of the puzzle with clues, similar to the ones below.

DOWN

2. What is guaranteed at Frank's Nursery, 49th St. and 54th Ave. N.?
3. "Rustler's _____ " is playing at the Garden Drive-In, Tyrone and Park.
4. What is located at 6980 54th Ave. N.?
5. Who was Northeast High School's opponent for football homecoming in 1985? 54th Ave. N. and 16th St. N.
6. What kind of products are sold at the Chevron Food/Gas Mart at 34th St. and 9th Ave. N.?
8. What type of trees are free at 33rd Ave. N. and Park St.?
10. What is free on the Shopping Center Construction Company sign at 49th St. and 9th Ave.?
11. Opposite of yes.
12. Greeting.
13. Laugh sound.
16. Who is going out of business at 34th St. N. and 16th Ave. N.?
17. Whose cottage is at 2605 50th Ave. N.?
18. Whose creamery milk is sold at 34th St. and 62nd Ave. N.?
19. What type of new homes are at 49th St. and 16th Ave. N.?

20. What type of puppies are sold at 49th St. and 3rd Ave. N.?

ACROSS

1. What position did John J. Murphy hold that is listed on the bronze plaque at 30th Ave. N. and 80th St. N.?
7. How many flavors does the Twistee Treat sell at 54th St. and 48th Ave. N.?
8. What night is bingo played at Holy Cross Church, 54th Ave. and 79th St. N.?
9. What is sweet at 62nd St. and Haines Road?
10. What does Lou sell at 34th St. and 32nd Ave. N.?
14. What costs $.85 at Farm Fresh Produce on 49th St. N. and 39th Ave. N.?
15. What costs $15,999 at Etnom Vans on the corner of 34th St. and 38th Ave. N.?
16. "To be or not to ____."
18. What has just arrived at Friedman's on 652nd Ave. N. and 60th St. N.?
21. Opposite of stop.
22. What Realty Company has the house for sale at _____ ?
23. Who is the assistant pastor at St. Luke's Church on 5th Ave. N. and 44th St.?

★ GIANT MONOPOLY

The whole youth group plays Monopoly using *real houses* around the community as the properties on the game board. Here's how it's played.

First, line up enough homes around town to be all the properties on the game board. If you want to cut down on the number of houses you use, have one house represent all the properties of the same color on the board. On the day or evening of the game, all the owners of these houses will need to be home and know what to do. In addition, cars and drivers for each team need to be arranged.

To play, use a regular Monopoly game. Divide into teams of four or five to ride in the same car. Distribute game money to each team as follows:

6 × $500 bills	15 × $ 10 bills
6 × $100 bills	15 × $ 5 bills
6 × $ 50 bills	15 × $ 1 bills
18 × $ 20 bills	

Place $1,000 in the middle of the board. Roll the dice to see which team goes first. Most of the regular Monopoly rules will apply, such as collecting $200 every time you pass Go. Here's where the game really differs—if you're the first one to land on a property, you may either buy it or, if you choose not to buy, allow it to go to the highest bidder. If someone owns the property you land on, then your team must get in the car and go to that property and pay the fee. The owners at the home will collect the fee and give you a receipt. Then, you return to the game so you can roll again. While you're gone, the other team can continue to play until they also have to leave for whatever reason. When there are other teams present at the game board, you must take your turn in order, but if no one else is there, you may roll more than once at a time. Here are some other rules.

1. *Chance or Community Chest:* You must pick a card and do what it says.

2. *Railroads:* You must get in the train car and go for a train ride— one mile out and one mile back. Then, you must pay the conductor (driver).

3. *Utilities:* You must go to the designated utility house and pay.

4. *Jail* You must go to jail if you land on the Go to Jail or draw Go to Jail. The jail can be a room in the building. You can get out of jail by paying $100, rolling doubles on your next turn, or sitting in jail for three minutes.

5. *Free Parking:* Landing on this gives you all the money in the middle of the board.

6. *Luxury Tax:* You pay $75 to the middle of the board.

7. *Income Tax:* You pay $200 to the middle of the board.

8. *Mortgages:* These are administered by the bank.

9. *Out of Money:* If you are running short on cash, you can take your title deed to your owner's house and collect your money, if there is any, at any time.

10. *Selling Property:* You may sell to another group or trade with them as you choose.

The game is over at the end of the designated time when each team must collect all its money and assets and turn them in to the bank. The team with the most money and accumulated property value wins. Playing a Monopoly game with the whole town as your playing board is crazy enough to generate a lot of enthusiasm and participation. Careful planning will insure its success.

★ HOT OR COLD CAR RALLY

This car rally is especially good with younger groups, like junior highers, and with the drivers, the adult sponsors. Only the drivers know the destination, and the passengers give their driver directions. Every five-tenths of a mile (or whatever distance you choose), the driver tells the passengers if they are getting warm or hot (near), cold or freezing (farther away) in relationship to the destination; however, he cannot tell them anything else until they have traveled another five-tenths of a mile. As a variation, the driver gives a clue once every two minutes, no matter how far they have traveled.

To avoid confusion in each car, have the riders elect a spokesperson for the group—the one who gives directions to the driver. All the passengers can have a voice in deciding which way to go, of course, but only the spokesperson can tell the driver where to go.

To avoid cars following each other, schedule each car leaving at intervals of five minutes. The time is recorded when they leave and when they reach the final destination. The best time wins.

★ MYSTERY CAR RALLY

The teams solve clues to read the prescribed route. Key words and numbers are left out of the instructions. Here are a few examples.

1. Turn right on _____ Street.

2. Take the first left after you pass _____.

3. Go _____ blocks and turn right.

Here are a few clues.

1. In the middle (answer: Central)

2. Three guys with energy (answer: Pep Boys)

3. 145 divided by 5 minus 14 plus 2 (answer: 17)

If a team gets the key word wrong, they'll get off course and it will cost them time, so give them a phone number to call if they do get lost and can't go any farther. Calling is a ten-minute penalty, however.

★ SPOTLIGHT CAR RALLY

Here's one that will attract a lot of attention. Rent a large spotlight (like those used at grand openings and carnivals) and place it at a hidden location to be the final destination for the car rally.

The starting point for the car rally should be just far enough away that the spotlight can be seen when it is beamed up into the sky.

All the cars leave at the same time, and the object is to be the first to arrive at the spotlight, which is beamed only once every two or three minutes for a couple of seconds. The teams need to watch carefully for it.

★ TIMED CAR RALLY

Following directions and enjoying the sights (if done during daylight hours) is the emphasis for this rally. Ahead of time, map out a rally course and write a detailed set of directions for each car. Cars should leave in five-minute intervals and be timed when they leave and when they return. The directions should include dozens of instructions like these:

1. Go east to the first stop sign.
2. Turn right.
3. At the traffic light, turn left, then go straight.
4. At the first traffic light, turn right.
5. Proceed under the trestle at 25 m.p.h.
6. Confirm water tower and the red-sided building on the left.
7. Turn left at the next stop sign.
8. Make a U-turn at the first opening in the middle divider.
9. Turn right at the stop sign.

After you map out the course, drive it yourself a few times and time it to find out how long it takes to follow the instructions exactly, obeying all the speed limits, then average all the times.

The object of the car rally is for the teams to match the official time for the course. They must follow the instructions exactly and obey all the traffic laws. The team closest to the official time wins.

★ TRUE/FALSE CAR RALLY

Give each team a list of instructions, like the ones below. The names are the names of the intersections; the statements after each one are either true or false. If the statement is true, they turn right at that intersection. If the statement is false, they turn left. Whichever team reaches the final destination in the shortest time possible wins. Plan your course ahead of time to have enough instructions (probably thirty or more) to keep them going for a while. No maps are allowed.

1. *Leave the Parking Lot:* In the Bible, Numbers is before Deuteronomy.

2. *At the Stop Sign:* Boston is the capital of Massachusetts.
3. *At Main Street:* Walter Payton plays for the Redskins.
4. *At Dempsey:* One gross is equal to 177.
5. *At Madison:* The Beatles got their start in Liverpool.
6. *At Broadway:* California has more people than New York.

★ WANDERLUST

This car rally is a lot of fun and can be done easily on bikes, as well as in cars. All the cars leave at the same time and may go in any direction the team charts on a map, which they are given at the beginning of the rally.

Whenever they come to an intersection (stop sign, signal, or cloverleaf), the team must decide which way to go by flipping two coins.

If both coins are heads, go right.

If both coins are tails, left.

If the coins are different, go straight.

To determine direction, you may use a die (one of a set of dice).

If you roll a 1 or a 2, go right.

If you roll a 3 or a 4, go left.

If you roll a 5 or a 6, go straight.

At the end of twenty flips of the coins or rolls of the die (twenty intersections), the team that gets the farthest away from the original starting place is the winner. In case there are some roads with no intersections, limit how far a team can go by disqualifying them if they can't return in a certain time.

As a variation, set a time limit, and the team that gets the farthest away at the end of the time limit, regardless of the number of intersections, is the winner. They'll have to make sure they stay within a safe returning distance.

★ CHAPTER FIVE ★

Other Hunts

This chapter contains a few extra hunts that are neither scavenger hunts, treasure hunts, nor car rallies—just fun to do!

★ **BARGAIN HUNTER**

Take your group to a local shopping mall or downtown area where there are lots of stores within walking distance. Then, divide into small groups and give each group a list, similar to the one below. Each group fills in the blanks by comparison shopping—finding the best bargains available for each item on the list—within a time limit. The group with the most items at the best prices wins. Here's a sample list.

1. A pair of size 12 snow boots
Store _____ Price _____

2. A one-pound box of candy turtles
Store _____ Price _____

3. A pair of men's briefs, size XL
Store _____ Price _____

4. The best laxative available, recommended by a druggist
Store _____ Price _____

5. A head gasket
Store _____ Price _____

6. A heart-shaped locket
Store _____ Price _____

7. Ten party balloons
Store _____ Price _____

BLUE GNU

Enlist five or six people who are strangers to your group. Assign each of them the name of a strange animal, like the Blue Gnu, the Pink Panda, and the Yellow Yak. The crazier the name, the better. Have each of these people wear an item of clothing that is the same color as the color in their assigned name when they go to a shopping center and mix in the crowd of shoppers.

In pairs, the hunters walk in the shopping center to find these crazy animals by asking direct questions. For example, they ask strangers, "Are you the Blue Gnu?" If when a person is questioned, the kids mention their activity, then the person automatically answers no, even if he really is the Blue Gnu. When the stranger answers yes, they write his real name down. The pair to list all the animals' real names wins.

★ BIGGER AND BETTER HUNT

Popular with many youth groups, the results of this activity are incredible. Everyone meets at a central location to be instructed and divided into small hunting groups of four or five, who hunt together on foot, in cars, or whatever way they can. Each group is given a penny to trade up for something better. For example, the group goes to someone's house and asks what in their house, excluding cash, they would trade for the penny. If the item is worth more than the penny, the group trades and thanks the people who made the trade and continues to trade whatever item they have for something bigger and better at the next house. Team members are not allowed to sweeten the pot by adding more money to the original penny or any of the items along the way.

Each team has a one-hour limit (or whatever time you decide) and then must return with the last item they traded for. The group with the Biggest and the Best is the winner.

This event has been done successfully with many different groups;

items, such as washing machines, television sets in working condition, even automobiles, have been the Biggest and Best. The collected items can be used later for a rummage sale or donated to a local service organization.

★ DIME DERBY

Here's a simple, challenging, and fun hunt. Divide into groups and give each group twenty dimes ($2.00). They must go to twenty different stores and buy twenty different items, each costing a dime or less and get a receipt for each purchase. Prizes are awarded on the basis of speed and variety of stores. A team can be the big winner by spending all twenty dimes in the fastest time and in stores that nobody else used.

MISSING-PARENT HUNT

Both the kids and their parents participate. First, call a meeting of the parents and explain that you have an activity that will help them relate to their teenagers, as well as be a lot of fun. The parents' role is to disguise themselves, so the kids in the youth group will not recognize them. Choose a very busy place, such as a large airport or shopping mall, and have them mill in the crowd, trying to be as inconspicuous as possible, but not actually hiding.

When a kid thinks he has found a parent, he must give the password "Mommy! Mommy!" or "Daddy! Daddy!," depending on the sex of the parent, so the parent will give him his signature. Whoever identifies the most parents within a time limit wins. Afterward, everyone meets for refreshments and awards are given to the parents for the Least-located Parent and the Best Disguise.

 SPY VS. SPY

Here's a special event that is perfect for small youth groups in cooperation with another youth group from a different church or organization. Both youth groups need to be about the same size.

Spy vs. Spy needs advance preparation. First, you need a photo of each entire youth group or individual photos of each person in the groups who is going to participate. About a week before the event, the two groups exchange photos to memorize the faces of the other group. Second, agree mutually upon a phrase, such as "You're under arrest!" for the kids to use when identifying each other. If you provide names with photos, a person can get extra points by saying the person's name, for example, "You're under arrest, Jennifer!"

On the given day or evening, the two youth groups go to a busy place, like a shopping mall or an airport, and meet at predetermined places; however, one group should not know the location of the other group. At a set time, the two groups disperse and try to locate each other within a time limit (thirty to sixty minutes), working individually or in pairs.

Whenever a kid thinks he has spotted someone from the other group, he runs to that person and says the key phrase. Whoever says this key phrase first gets points for his group. If a person is arrested three times, he must go to jail (or some predetermined place) and wait out the rest of the game there.

Plan a party afterward with refreshments, awards, and time for the two groups to get better acquainted.

CHAPTER SIX

Food Events

Events that feature food have always been popular with youth groups. Where would we be without old stand-bys like the potluck and the progressive dinner? Announce a pizza party or a Burger Bash and you've instantly captured the attention of any group of teenagers. As everyone knows, "the fastest way to a man's heart is through his stomach," but we sometimes forget that the old saying goes double with kids.

This chapter offers dozens of creative ways to eat together as a group or to provide food and refreshments for your activities, which will initiate a few crazy ideas of your own.

★ AWFUL WAFFLE PARTY

This idea can be used as a dessert, refreshment for some other activity, or all by itself. You'll need a few waffle irons and a huge batch of waffle batter. As the waffles come off the irons, provide various toppings—syrups, ice cream, nuts, jelly, peanut butter, whipped cream, and fruit. You might also want to include some awful toppings and dare kids to try them—pickles, onions, catsup, beets, or spinach.

★ BACKWARD PROGRESSIVE DINNER

As the name implies, this is a progressive dinner in reverse. Begin with dessert and a toothpick and work backward through the meal, with the last course being the appetizer or soup. To make it really interesting, try to do *everything* in reverse—travel backward, talk backward, sit in chairs backward, eat with plates upside down, and say grace at the last stop.

★ **BEFORE-SCHOOL BREAKFAST**

If your church is near a junior high or high school and if you have the facilities, here's a great idea for an outreach activity. Provide on a weekly basis a free Before-School Breakfast prepared by some of the youth sponsors or parents in the church. The breakfast can be simple (eggs, sausage, toast, donuts, and juice) and relatively inexpensive. Serve breakfast from 7:00–7:45 if school starts at 8 A.M. Call it a Prayer Breakfast if you choose to include prayer or Bible teaching. You'll be pleasantly surprised how well kids will respond to this activity.

★ BLUE-JEAN BANQUET

This is an informal banquet where the only acceptable dress code is blue jeans. An old barn or some other rural setting with wooden tables and bales of hay for seats is the best setting. Then, give awards for the oldest blue jeans, the dirtiest blue jeans, and the best-decorated blue jeans.

As a variation, plan an "Informal Formal," where the dress code is "If it looks good, don't wear it." Anything goes as long as it looks terrible. Give awards for the Worst-dressed Couple and most disgusting outfit. Something like this might make a crazy alternative to a prom night.

★ BUS BANQUET

Here's a unique idea for a banquet that's a great change of pace. Decorate the inside of a church bus to fit the occasion for the banquet— Christmas, Valentine's Day, Graduation. Save the back two seats for food. Have your adult sponsors be Flight Attendants or Trip Attendants and serve the food, as they do on airlines. The bus can cruise the city or take the group to an After-the-Meal Event, such as a concert or a play.

★ CAKE BAKE NIGHT

As a fund raiser or a service project, get the youth group together for an evening of baking and decorating cakes. Provide all the cake mixes and the cake decorating tools and group the kids into cake decorating teams. The cakes can be eaten, sold, or given away, depending on your objectives. Award prizes for the most creative, the craziest, and ugliest. You might want to combine this event with the ONCE-A-YEAR BIRTHDAY PARTY (p. 43); then, all the kids make birthday cakes for each month of the year.

★ CANDLELIGHT DINNER AT MCDONALD'S

This banquet idea can be done at any popular fast-food restaurant. Everyone meets at the restaurant in formal attire. Provide linen tablecloths, napkins, silverware, a centerpiece for each table (candles), and menus, like the one opposite. The front of the menu can include instructions, such as each person is limited to one hamburger, one order of fries or onion rings, and one drink per person. Even a separate wine list for all the beverage choices can be included.

After the tables are set and the kids seated, a waiter, who is dressed in a tuxedo, carrying a white linen napkin, takes everyone's order or collects the marked menus from everyone. The waiter also serves the food when it is ready.

For additional atmosphere, have a violinist play music. Try to make everything as pretentious as possible, and everyone will have a lot of fun. Be sure to get the restaurant management's permission ahead of time and give them the date of your activity. Normally, they will be happy to cooperate.

★ CANNED ICE CREAM

Here's a fun way to let your group make homemade ice cream. Divide into groups of four or five and give each group a one-pound and a three-pound metal coffee can with plastic lids. Provide each group a copy of the following recipe and let the fun begin.

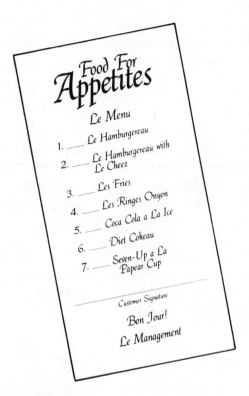

Food For
Appetites

Le Menu

1. _____ Le Hamburgereau

2. _____ Le Hamburgereau with Le Cheez

3. _____ Les Fries

4. _____ Les Ringes Onyon

5. _____ Coca Cola a La Ice

6. _____ Diet Cokeau

7. _____ Seven-Up a La Papear Cup

_____
Customer Signature

Bon Jour!

Le Management

1. In the one-pound can, mix together:

1 slightly beaten egg

1 cup milk

1 cup whipping cream

½ cup sugar

a dash of vanilla

2. Put the one-pound plastic lid on tightly. Place the one-pound can inside the three-pound can. Pack with crushed ice and 3/4 cup of rock salt. Put the three-pound plastic lid on tightly. Roll the can on the floor for fifteen minutes.

3. Drain the water and stir the ice cream. Replace lid, repack with ice and rock salt. Roll for five more minutes.

Add bowls and your favorite toppings, and you'll have some ice cream sundaes that will be hard to beat!

 COBBLER GOBBLER

This is a combination baking contest and scavenger hunt. Divide the group into teams of five, with boys and girls on each team. Each team is given a list of ingredients from a fruit cobbler recipe that they must find. When the teams collect all their ingredients, they report back to the church or wherever they will do the baking. The same cobbler recipe, except for the fruit, is given to each team and they prepare their cobbler for the oven.

While the cobblers are cooking, the group can play some games. When the cobblers are finished, a panel of judges tastes each one and awards prizes for the best tasting and most neatly prepared. Serve the cobblers to the group with ice cream.

 CREATIVE DINNER

Divide into groups, so each group has a car and access to some kitchen space. Give each group an amount of money, depending on your budget and the size of the group. Within a time limit, groups must bring back one part of the banquet, such as the appetizer, the drink, the main dish, the salad, the dessert, or the vegetable. They can choose whatever they want, but they must pay for it with the money provided. If the groups are not aware of what the others are bringing back, it will be a very interesting meal.

★ **DIME-A-DIP DINNER**

An oldie but goodie, this activity is not only a good banquet idea but also an excellent fund raiser. Plan a potluck-type dinner with all of the food donated by members of the group. Make sure you have enough salads, vegetables, main dishes, and desserts. Then, invite everyone to come and help themselves, paying a "dime a dip"—10 cents for every helping of each food they put on their plates, such as drinks, appetizers, butter, or rolls.

When used as a fund raiser for a particular project, usually there is a good turnout, and people eat heartily. You might want to set a certain minimum donation per person.

DO YOUR OWN DONUT

To break the cookie and Kool-Aid refreshment routine, start with several tubes of refrigerated powder biscuits. Form the biscuits into donut shapes and drop them into a skillet filled with one inch of cooking oil heated to 375 degrees. Turn when needed and remove when golden brown.

Provide a variety of toppings. Chocolate, vanilla, and peanut butter frostings work well. Sprinkles, coconut, and powdered sugar can be added on top of the frosting. Let each person make his own donut creation. Serve with hot chocolate in the winter for a pleasant way to warm up after an outdoor event. Whenever you plan it, have extra biscuit dough ready because the donuts go fast.

EAT, THINK, AND BE MERRY

Have a meal (eat), a study time (think), and a game time (be merry). By combining the three elements, you have a well-rounded evening and a name for it that's really catchy.

★ FAST-FOOD FOLLIES

Here's a delicious scavenger hunt idea. Have each person bring a specified amount of money, usually enough to handle a normal meal at a fast-food place. Divide into equal-sized teams to travel by car to various fast-food locations. Each team is given a list, like the sample one, adapted for the fast-food restaurants in your area.

A double hamburger from Wendy's
One scoop of chocolate ice cream from Baskin-Robbins
One hush puppy from Long John Silvers
One apple turnover from Burger Chef
One bag of French fries from Burger King
One hamburger from White Castle
One cheese dog from Der Weinerschnitzel
One taco from Taco Bell
One chicken leg from K.F.C.
One peanut butter shake from Dairy Queen
One liver or gizzard from Popeye's Fried Chicken
One Root Beer from A & W
One roast beef sandwich from Arby's
One burrito from Zantigo's
One Slurpee from Seven-Eleven
One soft drink from Frisch's

The team can pool their money and decide which team member eats which item at each location. When that person eats the specified item, he signs the list next to that item. Set a time limit, and the team that completes the list first or has the most items checked off is the winner.

★ FAST-FOOD FRENZY

This variation of FAST-FOOD FOLLIES is fun as well as a good lesson in budgeting. Each person starts with an amount of money that would buy a normal meal at most fast-food places. Teams pool their money and travel by car to a list of fast-food restaurants.

McDonald's

Burger King
Arby's
Taco Bell
Kentucky Fried Chicken
Orange Julius
Pizza Hut
Mr. Donut
Baskin-Robbins
Seven Eleven
Der Weinerschnitzel
Del Taco
Winchell's Donuts
Dairy Queen
Wendy's
Carl's Jr.

The group spends some money at each of the places on the list and returns with as little money as possible. They are not allowed to spend more than they are allowed per person but they must try to spend all of it, spreading it out over the entire list of restaurants. To add excitement, list about five different restaurants per person.

★ FAST-FOOD PROGRESSIVE DINNER

As the name implies, it's a progressive dinner, using various fast-food restaurants for each course of the meal. Let the kids decide on the route. If you travel in small groups, they can each take a different route but end up at the same place. Start with a salad at one restaurant, then move on to hors d'oeuvres (fries, soup, chili, or nachos). The main course can be hamburgers, tacos, or pizza, and the last stop is dessert.

For a slight variation, plan an Aggressive Dinner. The fast-food restaurants are each located in a different town. To add another variation, make it a Progressive-Aggressive Dinner using the same restaurant, like a Wendy's, in several different towns or communities within easy driving distance, so the kids would get a salad at one Wendy's, appetizers at another Wendy's in another town, and so on.

★ GET A LONG LITTLE DOGGIE

Check your local meat market to see if it is possible to order wieners up to ten feet long. Barbecue them on a long fire or bend them into a circle and cook them. There's something about cooking the World's Longest Hot Dog that has a lot of appeal to kids. Unless you can also find the World's Longest Bun, cut the wiener into individual portions to eat.

★ GIANT LOOKIE

A "lookie" is the name sometimes given to the gross-looking mess inside the mouth when someone is eating something and shows it to someone else. Unfortunately, that's where this idea gets its name.

Everyone brings a can of their favorite condensed soup and a can of their favorite soda pop. After everyone arrives, empty all the cans of soup into one large kettle, add the proper amount of water, then heat. Empty all the soft drinks into another large container. You will be surprised to find how good the punch and the soup taste, even when there's only one person who likes cream of asparagus.

★ GIANT PIZZA BREAKFAST

Here's an activity that is popular as well as attention-getting. Plan a Giant Pizza Breakfast either before church on Sunday or during the week before school. Serve frozen pizza and soft drinks. It's a great way to attract kids who wouldn't ordinarily attend your church or youth group functions.

★ HERITAGE DINNER

This potluck dinner allows kids to get in touch with their roots. Have each one bring a dish that represents his heritage or ancestry. If several nationalities are in his heritage, he can choose the most unusual.

In addition to the dish, the kids bring with them a family treasure or relic, photo, or other item of interest that reflects their heritage. The item need not be valuable, except for its story. Allow each person to tell as much as they know about their family roots. The kids could also bring baby pictures or travel posters of their homeland. Whatever the kids choose to bring makes an educational, as well as fun, activity.

INTERNATIONAL PROGRESSIVE DINNER

This event would be ideal for a dinner honoring foreign exchange students or emphasizing world missions. Similar to the HERITAGE DINNER (p. 121), each course of the meal is from a different country. At each location, add decorations, music, and other things that might add to that country's atmosphere.

Give each person a passport to be stamped at every location, as if the kids were actually traveling around the world. The passport can also be used as a program for the evening's activities.

 JUNK-FOOD POTLUCK

Here's a creative way to plan a potluck dinner that will have a special appeal to your youth group. Encourage your kids to bring generous amounts of their favorite junk food to share with others. Anything healthy or nutritious is not allowed. Be imaginative with the theme, and the kids will love it.

 LUCKY LUNCHES

For a quick after-church or before-the-event meal, ask everyone to bring a can of lunch food or a boxed meal, such as pizza or macaroni and cheese, with the label removed. If a can has the label painted on it or is particularly easy to recognize, disguise it in a lunch bag. No dog food, coffee grounds, pickle relish, or other less-than-tantalizing fare is allowed.

Number all the items, and the kids draw numbers to claim their lunches. The kids have fun discovering what they'll be eating; however, eating it can be a entirely different matter!

Provide some accompaniments to the meal, like chips, Jell-O, drinks, or a salad. Allow the kids to trade and share as they wish. As a variation, have your youth sponsors at stations, handing out each mystery course.

★ MYSTERY DINNER

Here's a classic food event, which has been used successfully for years and is always a winner.

Invite everyone to a Mystery Dinner at someone's home or at the church. After everyone arrives, each person is given a menu, which lists about twenty different items to be served. Name the menu items with nonsensical names, like the list below. The names can sound a little like the actual item, for example, White Slop might actually be a scoop of vanilla ice cream; the names may have no connection at all, for example Yippee Yahoo might actually be a pat of butter. The crazier the names, the better.

1. White Slop
2. Crunchy Crud
3. Thin and Flat
4. Yippee Yahoo
5. Nicey Slicey

All twenty items will be served to everyone, but *only in the order they choose*. On the menu, like the following one, are places to indicate which items each person wants for each course.

Have waiters or waitresses collect the menus after the kids have indicated their choices. Serve their first course, according to how they ordered, and the fun begins.

Some of the names on the list are actually things like the fork, the napkin, or a packet of mustard. Since the kids don't know what is what, they might order for their first course a baked potato, a scoop of ice cream, a stick of celery, a knife, and some raspberry jelly. To get their second course, they must finish their first course. All these surprises create a lot of fun.

Indicate below which items you would like served to you for each course.

FIRST COURSE

1. _____

2. _____

3. _____

4. _____

5. _____

THIRD COURSE

1. _____

2. _____

3. _____

4. _____

5. _____

SECOND COURSE

1. _____

2. _____

3. _____

4. _____

5. _____

FOURTH COURSE

1. _____

2. _____

3. _____

4. _____

5. _____

NEW-FASHIONED BOX SOCIAL

In the old-fashioned box social, the *girls* pack a box lunch for two, and the boys bid for them (like an auction) and share the lunch with the girl who packed it. The New-fashioned Box Social is just the opposite. The *boys* pack the lunch, and the girls do the bidding. With the right encouragement, some guys will bring fancy dishes, a tablecloth, candles, and soft music.

Combine this activity with a service project by having the girls bring canned goods to use as money in the bidding for the lunches. Then, the canned goods can be given to an organization for distribution to the poor.

 PIZZA HUNT

If there are lots of pizza restaurants where you live, try this hunt. Divide into teams to travel by car. Everyone leaves at the same time, goes to as many pizza places as possible within the time limit, and eats one pizza at each stop. This hunt teaches not only patience and where to find the best pizza in town, but also the value of phoning your order ahead.

 PIZZA SCAVENGER HUNT

Here's an unusual pizza party. Divide into teams and give each team a frozen pizza dough shell. Send them out in a residential area for sixty to ninety minutes, with no money. They must beg the necessary items (sauce, cheese) and the use of someone's oven to make the pizza. At the end of the time limit, the pizzas are brought back to the starting point for judging and eating. Scoring can include the first team back with a finished pizza, the best-tasting pizza, the most items on the pizza, or points awarded for certain kinds of items, such as pepperoni, anchovies, or hot peppers.

If your church has a big kitchen, use this simplified version. Give the kids a list of possible pizza items and tell them to bring back as many as they can find in the time limit. After the winners are determined, the pizzas can be made and baked as the grand finale to the evening's activities.

★ PERSONALIZED PIZZA PARTY

Provide kids with pizza dough and all the goodies that go on top and let them create their own personal pizzas. Each person gets a lump of dough to shape into a creative design; however, there must be a raised edge so the sauce won't run off. The pizza can be decorated with olives, mushrooms, cheese, pepperoni, and anchovies. While these creations are being baked, other games can be played. When they are ready, award prizes for originality and creativity. Then, eat!

 PROGRESSIVE DESSERT PARTY

As a variation of the Progressive Dinner, travel from one location to the next and sample a different dessert at each place. Make the portions small and serve a wide variety of desserts, such as ice cream, cake, pies, cookies, mousse, and cobbler. If you want to make everything chocolate, call it a Choco-holic Night.

 PROGRESSIVE DINNER HUNT

This activity combines a progressive dinner with a treasure hunt. Plan a treasure hunt, using the instructions and rules described in chapter 3. Teams solve clues, with one clue leading to the next. At each clue location, another course of the meal is served. The object is to complete the entire meal in the shortest amount of time. For best results, start each group at five or ten minute intervals and make sure they stay at each location for a certain amount of time to eat their food.

 RESERVATIONS ONLY

If your normal youth group activities suffer from poor attendance on those long holiday weekends (like Memorial Day and Labor Day), this idea might help.

Hold a Reservations-Only Dinner at the church, complete with linen tablecloths, lighted candles, music, and good food. This would be an excellent opportunity to get acquainted with members of your church from different ethnic backgrounds who can cook exotic foods. After dessert, show a video movie at someone's house.

Send out invitations two to three weeks in advance to give the event a sense of special importance. Ask everyone to R.S.V.P., and you'll find the kids will respond in a very positive way. Young people are looking for something good to do on the long weekend, and if you make a tradition out of it, you'll find that it will grow in popularity. It's an effective way to let your kids know that their local church remains active during the holidays.

★ ROAST THE PASTOR

Here's an event that can be a lot of fun for the whole church. Have the youth group sponsor a Roast-the-Pastor Banquet, like those seen on television when various people tell all kinds of jokes and secrets in the life of the honored guest. Of course, the pastor gets a chance for rebuttal. Have the kids work up lots of skits and crazy things to "roast" the pastor with. For example, you can take tapes of the pastor's sermons and splice them together to create a phony interview or a sermon that doesn't make any sense.

Serve roasted food, such as beef and corn. If you charge money for the meal, this event can be used as a fund raiser.

★ SCHOOL-LUNCH HAMBURGER SPECIAL

If you ever want to hear your kids use some of their more descriptive words, ask them about their school lunches. Since this subject usually causes all sorts of moans, groans, and weird expressions, conduct a contest to find which school in your area has the absolutely worst hamburger.

If you have kids from a variety of schools in your youth group, create an atmosphere of school spirit and competition. Have a representative from each school take a container to school, provided by the youth group, and bring back to the youth group an actual hamburger, purchased in the school cafeteria.

Then, let your panel of judges go to work. One at a time, they can examine, scrutinize, smell, taste, and perform chemical tests on each hamburger in front of the group. With a lot of creativity and some terrible cold and soggy hamburgers, this can be a lot of fun.

Meanwhile, have your own chefs cook some good hamburgers to show how it is really done. Promote it well, have the kids spread the word, and this event will really generate a lot of interest, enthusiasm, and disgust.

★ SNACK SEARCH

Snack Search is similar to BIGGER AND BETTER HUNT (p. 107). Divide the group into small teams of two or three. Give each team a sack lunch with a variety of not-very-edible items, such as an onion, a lemon, a jar of baby food, a can of dog food, a can of evaporated milk, soup mix, or bird seed.

Each team goes into the neighborhood and trades up one item at a time to improve the quality of their lunch within a time limit. They cannot go to any of their own homes nor can they buy anything. They may only trade one item for another at any one location.

You'll be amazed at the new lunches—sandwiches, watermelons, pies, all sorts of goodies. When everyone has returned, each team displays their new lunch. An award can be given to the most improved. . After judging, chow down!

★ SOCIAL GRACES

Good manners are making a comeback! Many young people feel like complete idiots when they go on their first big date or attend a formal dinner for the first time because they don't know how to act. So, organize a special banquet, planned and arranged by the youth group to teach some of the social graces to your kids in a fun, non-threatening way. Part of the program can be done tongue-in-cheek, but overall it should be a serious attempt to help kids feel confident when they find themselves in a formal social setting.

Before the banquet, divide the group into committees, each researching etiquette on table manners, serving, introductions, seating, decorations, and table setting. Then put the committees to work in their areas getting the room ready before the banquet. Appoint a couple of guys to be hosts.

As the kids arrive, they are greeted by the hosts. Girls are seated properly by their hosts or dates, practicing several times taking off their coats gracefully and sitting without awkwardness. Before the meal, the hosts briefly discuss how to make restaurant reservations, how to enter a restaurant, how to use the napkin, and how to read the menu and order.

When the first course (soup) is served, have a group quickly explain proper etiquette for eating soup, what to do with crackers, which spoon to use, and where to place the spoon. Everyone practices during the course.

Next is salad. A couple of kids explain how to properly cut the lettuce, what fork to use, how to eat a cherry tomato, and how to handle olive pits and bread sticks.

For a main course, try chicken, baked potatoes, rolls and butter. Groups can explain how to manage these foods and how to complain gracefully to a waiter if something is wrong. After the main course, there can be a short program, speaker, or entertainment.

Finally, dessert is served, and again, practical matters are discussed.

Topics include tough pie crust, drips and crumbs, what to do with the napkins or if something falls on the floor, tipping, paying for the check, and how to leave the table. In addition to being helpful for the kids, parents will love it. With a little creativity, it can be a lot of fun, too.

 SOUP-ER SUNDAY

Here's a good food event for Super Bowl Sunday. Have all the kids get together to watch the game and cook a big pot of soup. You can either fix a recipe you know the kids will enjoy or have each person bring his favorite can of soup and mix them all together. Provide some fresh-baked bread and a beverage, and you'll be all set for a Soup-er Sunday.

★ **SPAGHETTI SLOBFEST**

This banquet idea will keep your kids laughing now and later. Set up tables and assign places at the tables for everyone. Set the tables with the most unusual eating dishes and utensils you can find. For example, one person may have to eat out of a vase with a wooden spoon. Another person eats out of a coffee creamer with an ice cream scoop. Someone else gets a fruit jar and chopsticks. Make each place setting as crazy as possible. Then, cover everything with a sheet. Seat the entire group at the same time. When everyone is seated, remove the sheets and watch the looks on their faces.

Get your camera ready. The hosts can serve the spaghetti, and the kids are instructed to eat only with the utensils provided. You can also serve bowls of salad and some bread. It will be a banquet they'll remember for a long, long time, especially when you show the pictures later.

★ SUNDAY-SCHOOL TAILGATE PARTY

Tailgate parties have become very popular at sports events in the past few years. People come hours before the game in their motor homes, cars, campers, or pick-up trucks and cook hamburgers, visit, and toss a football around. So, try a tailgate party for your church.

Have everyone come an hour or two early to Sunday school and cook breakfast over a hibachi or campstove. Serve coffee and orange juice, sausage and eggs, and pancakes. People can bring lawn chairs,

Frisbees, guitars, and just relax and have a good time before it's time for Sunday school.

One church has made this an annual event and advertises their tailgate party a few weeks in advance. Lots of people come who normally don't attend Sunday school. It has become a favorite special event for the entire church.

★ **SUNDAE NIGHT SOCIAL**

Here's a great way to put new life into the old ice cream social. Invite families as well as the youth groups to come for an evening of fun. Provide a variety of ice cream toppings.

After everyone arrives, divide into teams with names like these:
1. The Chocolate Chips
2. The Strawberries
3. The Pistachio Nuts
4. The Rocky Roads
5. The French Vanillas

Then, play some games like these:

1. *You Scream, I Scream, We all Scream for Ice Scream:* Each team creates a cheer based on the name of their team. The winner can be judged on creativity, originality, humor, and choreography.

2. *Cherry-Topper Relay:* Each team lines up single file with everyone having one bare foot. Place a chair about twenty feet from the team line with a pan of crushed ice, water, and several maraschino cherries in it and an empty sundae dish close-by. Each contestant runs down, sits in the chair, fishes out the cherry with his bare toes, places it in the sundae dish, and races back to tag the next player, who repeats the same activity. First team to get all their cherries in the dish is the winner.

3. *Banana Peel:* Get the captain of each team to take off his shoes and socks and sit facing the audience. Give each captain a banana to peel using only his feet. The first one to succeed is the winner.

4. *Nut-Cracker Relay:* Each team member places a peanut between his knees, waddles to a sundae dish about ten feet away, and drops the peanut into it. If he misses, he picks up his peanut and gets back in line to try again. If he drops his peanut before reaching the dish, he goes back to the starting line to begin again. The team with the most peanuts in the dish within a time limit is the winner.

5. *Ice-Cream-Cone Carry:* Place a chair about thirty feet from each line. The first player on each team walks to the chair, goes around it, and comes back while balancing an empty ice cream cone on top of his head. If it falls, he puts it back on and keeps going. If it breaks, he gets a new one. First team to have everyone complete the task successfully is the winner.

After all the games, serve ice cream to everybody and have them make their own sundaes from all the toppings. As a variation, create the World's Largest Sundae in a large pan in the middle of the room, covered with all kinds of toppings, nuts, and whipped cream. Give everyone a bowl and a spoon and let them dig in.

★ WORLD'S GREATEST FRENCH FRY

This activity allows your kids to become critics or reviewers of the things they consume. The object is to find the very best French fry in the city. The kids go from one fast-food restaurant to another and try their French fries. Each member rates the fries on predetermined qualities, such as taste, appearance, cost, amount of fries per serving, and saltiness. To add a professional touch, have each member eat a cracker before they taste to "wash the palate." The group's ratings and any additional comments can be shared in the church bulletin. Any common food item works as well.

★ WORLD'S LARGEST BANANA SPLIT

Here's one that a lot of youth groups have done with great success. To make the World's Largest (or Longest) Banana Split, get a long section of house rain gutter. You may have to plug the ends of it to keep it free from leaks. Line the gutter with heavy duty aluminum foil about three times.

Now you're ready to make the banana split. Provide ice cream, bananas, toppings, nuts, and whipped cream. Arrange to have everyone eat out of the same boat or dip out individual servings into plastic containers, obtained at a local dairy store. Be sure to take pictures.

 WORLD'S LARGEST POPCORN BOWL

Next time you have a movie night at your church or want a different refreshment for your next special event, try this. Announce ahead of time that you will have the World's Largest Popcorn Bowl at the activity. The kids will come just to see if you can deliver.

Get lots of popcorn popped. For the bowl, use a molded plastic, child-sized swimming pool. Just fill it with popcorn, and it will indeed be the world's largest. The kids will love it.

 WORLD'S LARGEST SUBMARINE SANDWICH

Order from a bakery the longest loaf of bread they can make, which is usually seven to ten feet long. Have all the kids in your group bring their favorite kinds of lunch meat and cheese. Have condiments, mayonnaise, and sandwich spread. Let the kids pack the loaf and cut off as much as they can eat when it is finished. Surprise the kids with this snack after a trip to the beach or some other event that makes them really hungry.

CHAPTER SEVEN

Sports Events

This chapter contains a variety of special events that are patterned after sports events and similar to the Theme Events in chapter one. These events are especially featured here because their common theme is competitive sports.

You can easily create your own sports or game events if you have a few good games and a good place to play them, such as an open field, a gymnasium, or someone's backyard. Get a group of kids together and play any of the games in our book *Play It!* (by Rice and Yaconelli, Zondervan/Youth Specialties, 1986). Give your event a crazy name to create plenty of interest and anticipation. For example, if you call it a R.I.O.T. (Ridiculous, Idiotic, Odd, but Terrific), you can be sure that the kids will be there in force. Play a variety of games—mixers, team games, and relays—and end with refreshments or perhaps a special program, such as music, skits, or a speaker. Whatever the combination, it is a very effective special event for any youth group.

Here are some unique sports events that are always fun.

★ ALL-CHURCH OLYMPICS

As a great family event, have your youth group sponsor a Summer Olympics for the entire church. Organize an Olympic Committee to schedule all the events, which can take place all on one day or over several weeks. An Opening Ceremony can kick things off, and a Closing Ceremony can wrap things up. Provide awards (gold, silver, and bronze medals) for the winners in each event. Divide the entire congregation into nations, who decide the participants in each competition.

Events can include both individual and team competition—volleyball, racquetball, tennis, pool, bowling, tug of wars, Frisbee throwing, cow chip tossing, or anything you can imagine. Older folk can participate in horseshoes, darts, and similar activities; children can participate in relays, bike riding, and other events like these. What a good way to perk up a dull summer and draw the entire congregation closer together!

★ **BAT-AND-PUTT NIGHT**
If you have a Family Fun Center in your area with a miniature golf course and batting cages, rent the location for a couple of hours for a special Bat-and-Putt Night sponsored by your youth group.

To spice up the fun, encourage some competition by guaranteeing special prizes for all the winners. Divide the youth into different competitive levels (junior-high boys, junior-high girls, senior-high boys, senior-high girls), so each person competes with those on his own level. The competitions can be arranged in several categories.

Golf:
1. Best golf score for a whole round
2. Most holes in one
3. Best score left- or wrong-handed
4. Worst score on any one hole
5. Worst score on a whole round

Batting:
1. Most hits in 25 tries for each speed
2. Most consecutive hits
3. Ugliest swing of the night

4. Best batting average overall
5. Home runs

★ **BIKE RODEO**

Have your kids bring their bikes to a large open area for a variety of games like these:

1. *Calf Roping:* One kid stands in the center of an open area, and each contestant tries to "rope the calf" as he rides by on a bicycle. After a rider successfully lassos the person in the middle, he should immediately drop the rope to avoid injury to himself or the calf. The calf may duck but he must keep his hands at his side and stay on his feet. The fastest time wins.

2. *The 100-Yard Crawl:* Bikes must travel in a straight line to a finish line that is one hundred yards away as slowly as possible. If a rider touches a foot or any part of his body to the ground, trying to maintain his balance, or goes off course, he is disqualified. The la... person to finish is the winner.

3. *Bike Cross-Country:* This event is an obstacle course that can include anything you want. The rougher the trail, the better. Plan a Long Jump (a four-inch log that the biker and bike must jump over), a Tight Rope (a ten-foot-long 2 x 4 that the biker and bike must stay on), a Limbo Branch (low tree branch that the bike rider must go under on his bike), and a Tire Weave (slalom course made from old tires). From a starting point, bikes compete for time.

4. *100-Yard Spring:* This is a regular 100-yard dash from a standstill with bikes.

5. *Bike Pack:* See how many can fit on a bike and still go ten feet.

6. *Backward Race:* Kids who know how to ride a bike backward race down a 100-yard track.

7. *Bike Jousting:* Arm two kids with water balloons. They ride toward each other on two parallel tracks and try to hit the other rider with the water balloon as they ride by.

8. *Barrel Race:* Set up several barrels (or other markers) in a figure-eight course. Bike riders try to ride around the barrels in the fastest time.

9. *Freestyle:* Have kids compete for the most creative, most difficult, most impressive freestyle bike ride. Judges can determine the winners.

★ **GUINNESS GAMES**

As an annual event for your youth group, schedule a contest day when kids try to set a world's record like those in the *Guinness Book of World Records*. Instead of competing against the Guinness Book, kids compete against themselves and try to set a new Personal World Record each year, so the first year, the records are set, and each subsequent year, kids try to break them. Here are a few suggested contests.

Eating Contests (amount of food eaten within time limit):
1. Hamburgers
2. Tacos
3. Sloppy Joe's
4. Marshmallows
5. Slices of pizza
6. Lemon wedges
7. Onions
8. Bananas

Endurance Contests (timed):
1. Standing on your head
2. Running in place
3. Telling jokes
4. Stare down
5. Pogo-stick jumping
6. Dribbling a basketball
7. Keeping eyes open without blinking

Skill Contests:
1. Free-throw shooting (consecutive)
2. Frisbee throwing (distance)
3. Marshmallow throwing (distance)
4. Belching (loudest, number in succession)
5. Bubble blowing (biggest, number in succession)
6. Various games (highest score)

Other Contests:
1. Phone-booth stuffing (number of kids inside)
2. Hula-hoop packing (number of kids inside)
3. Marshmallows-in-mouth stuffing (number)

There can be a separate boys' and girls' category in the athletic events. Kids pay an entry fee and sign up for whichever event they would like to try or they can invent their own category, where they think they can set a record. Present trophies to the New World Record Winners and post a chart for the year with all the winners listed.

★ GOOFY GOLF

Here's a unique miniature golf tournament. Build your own miniature golf course, using buildings, rooms, and hallways in your church. Go to a sporting goods store or a golf-pro shop and purchase nine (or eighteen) tin putting cups. Obtain enough putters and golf balls for everyone.

Design the course by marking (with tape or with small carpet samples) the tees for each hole. The holes can be as long or as short as you want, go in and out of rooms, down hallways, up ramps, down staircases, and everywhere. Create some water hazards, traps, and tunnels. If you can get some old 2 x 4's, use these for marking the fairways and banking the balls.

Let the kids choose foursomes for tournament competition. Provide score cards, just like the pros. As an option, draw a map of the course, including distances to the holes and pars for each hole.

If you do not have carpeted floors, use stale marshmallows or Ping-Pong balls, instead of regular golf balls. Following the tournament, you can serve Iced Tee, Club Sandwiches, Chip Shots (potato chips), and Holes-in-One (donuts).

★ **LATE GREAT SKATE**

Arrange to rent a roller rink for your private use or find a large, flat open area where kids can skate. Make sure everyone has some skates. If at the roller rink, ask to plan your own skating program and consider an all-night event that starts around midnight and lasts until dawn. Roller rinks are easier to rent at such a ridiculous hour.

Play all sorts of games on skates. Many regular outdoor or indoor games, especially relays, can be played on skates, giving them an added dimension of fun. Be careful to organize games that are not too rough to avoid possible injuries.

Here are a few sample games that can be played on skates.

1. *Rag Tag:* Everyone gets a rag that hangs out of his back pocket or out of his pants. At a signal, all skate in the same direction, and each skater tries to grab someone else's rag without having his taken. Once his rag is gone, that skater is out of the race. Awards are given to whoever grabs the most rags and to whoever manages to stay in the game the longest.

2. *Obstacle-Course Relay:* Set up an obstacle course for everyone to skate through, one at a time. The first team to have each of its skaters complete it is the winner.

3. *Triple Skate:* Especially good as a mixer; everyone skates around the rink in threes. No passing is allowed. At a signal, the skater in the middle, or on his right or left, moves up to the next threesome.

4. *Scooter Race:* Have one kid on his haunches who is pushed by another skater. Set a number of laps for the race.

5. *Tumbleweed:* This event is very tiring for the skaters. Have them squat when the music stops or when the whistle blows.

6. *One-Legged Race:* Skaters race with only one skate on, using the other foot to push.

7. *Run the Gauntlet:* Girls line up in two parallel lines, and the boys skate between them with balloons tied to their seats. The girls try to pop the balloons with rolled up newspapers as they skate by. As a variation, put clothespins on the boys' backs, and the girls try to grab them as the boys skate by. Awards are given to the girl who grabs or pops the most and to the boy who lasts the longest.

8. *London Bridge:* Two skaters stand opposite each other, grab hands, and form a bridge. Each team lines up. At a signal, they skate under the bridge as many times as possible before the time limit is up. Station a counter by the bridge. The team that has the most skaters pass under the bridge is the winner.

There are many more possibilities. For breathers, show some films, serve refreshments, or present a special program.

★ ODD-BALL OLYMPICS

Organize a crazy indoor track meet using events, like those below. To add to the fun, divide the kids into countries and have them choose a national anthem (any song they wish) to be sung whenever their country wins an event. Plan an elaborate opening ceremony, complete with the lighting of a torch. Award gold, silver, and bronze medals on a three-tiered platform while the winner's anthem is being sung at a closing ceremony.

1. *The Discus Throw:* Paper plates are thrown for distance. If outdoors, use Frisbees or cow chips.

2. *The Hammer Throw:* Each contestant throws an inflated paper sack tied onto a thirty-inch piece of string. Holding the loose end of the string, each contestant swings that sack around his head several times before throwing for distance.

3. *The Javelin Throw:* Contestants throw toothpicks (or pencils, knitting needles, or straws) like javelins. With the throwing arm back and the other arm out in front for balance, he takes three running steps and throws as far as possible.

4. *The Shot Put:* Competitors throw an inflated balloon or water balloon for distance, shot-put style.

5. *The 440-Relay:* Almost any relay can be played. For a good one, have the entire team leapfrog over each other around a circular course.

6. *The High Jump:* Play a game of Electric Fence in which the entire team goes over a wire or pole, which keeps getting higher and higher. They can get over any way they want with teammates' help, but once over, they can't come back to the other side until all their teammates are over. The last person has real difficulty getting over the fence, since there is no one left to help him.

★ **PAPER AIRPLANE DERBY**

Here's an easy special event that's a lot of fun. Ask all the kids to bring their own paper airplanes. Kids can use paint, glue, and paper, but no wire, wood, or metals. Feature these creations during an evening of games. Give awards for the best designed airplane, the largest airplane, the smallest airplane, the farthest flight, the plane that stays in the air the longest, the most accurate flight through a hoop, and best landing on a runway.

★ **OLYMPIC MARATHON**

This Olympic-style event generates a lot of excitement. The marathon should be designed so each person on each team has the same number of opportunities to participate in a complicated relay where each contestant does something different. Organize the group into countries (teams) and give each team a copy of the Marathon Route, like the one below.

The directions on the Marathon Route must be followed precisely in order. A banana is used as a baton. Let each team go separately and time each one. The rest of the team stays with the participants in action, cheering them on. To begin, have each team fill in the blanks with the names of the people on their team.

Here is a sample Marathon Route, which is done inside a church building.

Instructions:

These events must be done in order. You cannot begin until you receive your banana. No running is allowed unless the event specifies that running is permitted. Fast walking is okay. If you run while inside the church building, you will have to start your event over.

1. _____ rides tricycle from starting point to the curb line at the alley (passes baton to next contestant).

2. _____ walks on stilts to first door of C.E. building (passes baton).

3. _____ sits on top stair by the door and goes down to the basement, one step at a time on his seat. At the bottom of the stairs, he picks up a matchbox with his nose and hops on his left foot through the

first door on the right to where his teammate is. He passes the matchbox from his nose to his teammate's nose (passes banana, too).

    4. _____ who just got the matchbox on his nose, says loudly and distinctly (so everyone can hear):

> Peter Piper picked a peck of pickled peppers.
> A peck of pickled peppers Peter Piper picked.
> If Peter Piper picked a peck of pickled peppers,
> Where's the peck of pickled peppers Peter Piper picked?

(passes baton).

    5. _____ and _____ do a wheelbarrow race from that point to the door of room 103. The baton can ride on the back of the wheelbarrow (passes baton).

    6. _____ goes into room 103, picks up the broom, holds it straight up against his chest, looks up at it, and turns around it rapidly twenty times in succession, sets it down on the ground, and jumps over it (passes baton).

    7. _____ runs to the blackboard in room 106, draws a picture of an elephant, and signs his name (passes baton).

    8. _____ stands at the bottom of the stairs and eats one-half of a peanut butter sandwich, no drinks allowed. He then recites the Pledge of Allegiance (passes baton).

    9. _____ leaves the building, runs across the parking lot to the basketball court, picks up the basketball on the court, and makes five baskets in a row (passes baton).

    10. _____ goes into the men's restroom next to the youth office and gets a roll of toilet paper. He then wraps up _____ and the banana in the entire roll like a mummy. The mummy runs down the hallway to the church library, where his teammates remove all the paper and put it in the trash can (passes baton).

    11. _____ grabs the paper sack on the first table in the library, takes the clothes out of the sack, and puts them on over his own clothes. Carrying the sack, he then runs around the sanctuary to the corner of

Main and Thomas streets and takes off the clothes and puts them back in the sack (passes baton).

12. _____ takes the sack of clothes and returns them to the library table. On the book return counter, he takes the envelope containing fifty cents, buys a Coke from the machine, and drinks it all (passes baton).

13. _____, _____, _____, _____, _____, and _____ (6 team members) form a pyramid. The person on the top peels the banana and eats it without falling.

★ **SPOONS TOURNAMENT**

There are many popular games, which can be used as the basis for a major tournament. Spoons (sometimes called Donkey) is such a game. Here's how to play Spoons.

A small group of kids (any number from four to ten) get in a circle, either on the floor or around a table. In the middle are several ordinary spoons (coins, bean-bags, or anything that can be grabbed)—one less than the number of players in the circle. The spoons can be arranged in a circle, like the spokes of a wheel, with the handles pointing out at the players.

A regular deck of playing cards is needed; however, you will only use a few of the cards. Each person gets four-of-a-kind of one card. If there are six players, for example, then you will use six different cards but all four suits of those six cards (24 cards total).

To begin the game, shuffle the cards thoroughly and deal them out, so each player has four cards, not necessarily four-of-a-kind. The dealer (a different dealer for each round) announces which direction cards will be passed—right or left. If he announces right, then when he says go, each player passes one card from his hand to the person on his right and receives a card from the person on his left. If he doesn't want the card he has received, he continues passing it to his right, receives a new one from the left, and so on. Cards keep being passed around, one at a time, to the right until someone gets four-of-a-kind in his hand.

When a person gets four-of-a-kind, he silently (sneakily) grabs one of the spoons. Then, everyone else grabs a spoon, but someone cannot get a spoon, since there is one less spoon than people. Whoever fails to grab a spoon either is out of the game or gets one letter of the word "donkey." When anyone gets all the letters, he's out.

Once the kids are familiar with the game, organize a Spoons Tournament and offer prizes to the winners. It's so crazy and enjoyable, the kids may want to make it an annual event. Start the preliminary rounds in a large room with four or more teams of five or more kids on each team. Have each team eliminate people, one at a time, until only two are left from each team. Those two will be the team representatives in the finals. Have the finalists sit around a special regulation table with spotlights shining directly on the game. Someone in a referee shirt shuffles the cards, makes judgment calls, and does whatever he can to enhance the drama of competition. Present a team trophy and individual awards as well.

★ SUPER BOWL BASH

If your youth group likes watching professional football, plan a party on Super Bowl weekend featuring some football films, refreshments, and games like these:

1. *The Super Bowl Bible Quiz:* Prepare a list of Bible questions ahead of time. Divide into two teams and score touchdowns by answering eight questions correctly. Each question is worth ten yards. Teams on offense start on the 20-yard line and have eighty yards to go for a touchdown. A team keeps the ball as long as they answer questions correctly. When the ball goes to the other team, they begin where they were on their last possession. After each question, the team can huddle and then make their play (answer the question). When a team scores, then both teams start over on their 20-yard lines for the next series of downs. Play for as long as you like.

2. *Coin Flip Football:* Have the kids pair off and give each pair a gridiron printed on a piece of paper like the one below with these rules.

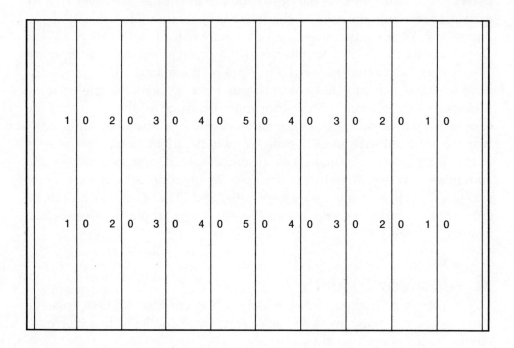

a. Flip a coin to see who receives first. Start on your 20-yard line.
b. Advance the ball ten yards for every heads you flip.
c. Lose ball to other player for two tails flipped twice in a row.
d. Kick ball forty yards if you change offense to another player.
e. First player to score two touchdowns is the winner.

3. *Super Bowl Bingo:* Distribute bingo games, similar to the one shown on next page. Ahead of time, write your own questions in the spaces, using the current Super Bowl teams. The kids mill about the room, asking people to answer the questions on their sheets. Whenever someone knows or thinks he knows the answer, he tells that person his answer and signs his name in the space. The first person to get five in a row wins if the five people can answer correctly the questions they signed.

★ TIN MAN TRIATHLON

Here's a scaled down version of the famous Iron Man Triathlon. Advertise it not only as a test of endurance but also an opportunity for the group to help one another accomplish a tough goal. Promote participation with Tin Man T-shirts, buttons, and posters.

Any high schooler can enter one event or all three. The course should be challenging, such as a half-mile swim, a twenty- to thirty-mile bike ride, and a two to four-mile run. Emphasize helping one another finish the course. It shouldn't be too grueling if they spend a couple of weeks conditioning; however, have a nurse, salt pills, and water available.

Top off the day with an awards ceremony, a good meal, and a special program, perhaps featuring a professional athlete as a guest speaker.

★ TURKEY BOWL

The next time you're planning events around the football bowl games, beat the rush by hosting your own Turkey Bowl over the Thanksgiving holidays.

The Turkey Bowl is a football game played by your youth group (boys and girls) or with another youth group in your town. It should be touch, flag, or Flamingo football (boys play on one leg).

More than just a game, make the Turkey Bowl a special event by

SUPER BOWL BINGO
Two Player Game

What was the '84 Super Bowl score?	How many games did the 49ers win in their regular season?	What is Walter Payton's football jersey number?	Who is in today's Super Bowl?	What emblem do the Bears have on their helmets?
How many games did the Dolphins win in their regular season?	Who is the Chicago Bears' head coach?	Which NFL team has had a perfect season?	With which team did Joe Namath win a Super Bowl?	In what city is today's Super Bowl being played?
What NFL team has the most famous cheerleader?	What team plays in Indianapolis?	Put your own name here!!	How much does one minute of commercial time cost for this Super Bowl?	Who is the Dolphins' quarterback?
Who is the 49ers' coach?	Which team is going to win the 1986 Super Bowl?	Who is the Dolphins' coach?	Name four other bowl games.	Where is Dan Marino's former college?
Where did Joe Montana play college football?	Name three coaches for the Bears— past or present.	Who won last year's Super Bowl?	Who won the 1984 Super Bowl?	Who is the Cowboys' coach?

having a Bowl Breakfast to kick off the day. Invite parents to this light breakfast and plan a special program, featuring a local coach as speaker.

Give this event lots of publicity and create a special Turkey Trophy for the winning team.

CHAPTER EIGHT

Seasonal Events

Here are some great socials and special events that are especially appropriate for the various seasons and holidays of the year. For other ideas, see our book *Holiday Ideas for Youth Groups* (by Rice and Yaconelli, Youth Specialties/Zondervan, 1981).

The New Year

★ BIRTH OF A NEW YEAR'S PARTY

The COME-AS-YOU-WERE PARTY (p. 24), with its theme of babies, is a great way to start the New Year.

★ NEW-YEAR'S-EVE EVE PARTY

With the holidays becoming more and more dangerous on New Year's Eve, plan a New-Year's-Eve Eve Party instead. Celebrate New-Year's-Eve Eve at midnight the night *before* New Year's Eve just like you would on New Year's Eve. The kids can have all the fun of New Year's Eve and then stay home to baby-sit on the *real* New Year's Eve.

The Winter Months

★ WINTER OLYMPICS

If you happen to be fortunate (or unfortunate) enough to live in an area where it snows, a Winter Olympics can be a great event for youth groups. Find a place with plenty of room to play, as well as plenty of snow, and play some of these games.

1. *Three-Man Ski Race:* Using a pair of custom-made three-man skis, have teams of three race against each other, against the clock, or relay-style. For safety, do this only on a flat ("cross-country") course, not downhill.

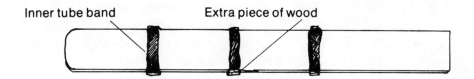

Inner tube band   Extra piece of wood

Three-man skis are made out of one-inch thick, 6-inch by 6-foot boards. With the front end rounded, use three bands of inner tube (bicycle inner tubes work great) for the footholds. Secure the bands to the side of the ski with an extra piece of wood to prevent the rubber from tearing at the nail. Make sure you have the bands tight enough across the ski to hold the booted foot. Keep an extra band or two and a hammer and nails handy.

2. *Stilt Relay:* Have each team member see how far he can go on a pair of stilts in one minute, then the next team member tries for one minute, and the competition continues. The team to get the farthest is the winner. (Don't do this one in deep snow.)

3. *Sled Spring:* One person (usually the smallest) sits on a sled, while the rest of the team pulls him with a twenty-foot rope. The race course can be straight up and back, or obstacle filled.

4. *Snow Mountain:* Teams compete to make the highest mountain of snow in five minutes.

5. *Snowball Throw:* Kids throw snowballs for distance, aiming at adult sponsors just out of range, and accuracy, throwing through a tire or some other object.

6. *Snow Sculpturing:* Each team sculptures something out of snow. Assign a theme or let the kids create anything they want, coloring it with food coloring.

7. *Snowmobile Slalom:* While being pulled behind a snowmobile on a giant inner tube, team members try to grab flags stuck in the snow, without falling off the tube. Keep a safe speed.

8. *Snowshoe Race:* Run a relay race on snowshoes.

9. *Inner-Tube Races:* If you have a good slope, schedule timed inner-tube races down the hill. Competition can include singles, doubles, or an entire team with tubes tied together in a chain.

 SNOWMOBILE RALLY

Try one of the scavenger hunts, treasure hunts, car rallies or progressive dinners, which are normally done in cars, on snowmobiles.

Groundhog Day

 GROUNDHOG BANQUET

Do something really different. Plan a Groundhog Banquet on Groundhog Day (Feb. 2). With a little creativity, this could be the highlight of the year! Generate a lot of interest and excitement with your promotions. The Chamber of Commerce in Punxsutawney, Pennsylvania (where Groundhog Day originated) will send you some colorful brochures about the history of Groundhog Day. Souvenir ground-hog statues, glasses, notepaper, decals, pennants, and all kinds of good ground-hog memorabilia are also available from them. Their address is 123 S. Gilpin, Punxsutawney, PA 15767; their phone (814) 938–7700.

For your banquet, serve dishes, like Groundhog Stew or Ground-hog Pie. Stage a Shadow-casting Contest to see which contestants can create the most interesting shadows against the wall (use a slide projector for light). Play some games with groundhog names, such as Groundhog Relay or Catch the Groundhog. Sing some Groundhog carols, like those below.

"I'm Dreaming of the Great Groundhog"

I'm dreaming of the Great Groundhog
Just like I do this time each year.
When he brings nice weather
And brings us together
To wait for him to appear.

I'm dreaming of the Great Groundhog
With every Groundhog card I write.
May your Groundhog's Day be bright
When the Great Groundhog visits you tonight.

"Groundhog Wonderland"

Groundhogs hoot, are you list'ning?
'Neath the sun, all is glist'ning
A real warm sight, we're happy tonight
Waitin' in a Groundhog Wonderland.

In the field, we're watching for the groundhog.
We've been waiting for this day all year.
Do you think that he will see his shadow?
And will we know if springtime's almost here?
Later on, while we're eating
What we got on Groundhog Day

We'll share all our sacks
Of good groundhog snacks
Waitin' in a Groundhog Wonderland.

"Deck the Field"

Deck the field with brown and black
Fa la la la la la la la la.
Take along your goody sack
Fa la la la la la la la la.
Don we now our groundhog apparel
Fa la la la la la la la la.
Toll the ancient groundhog carol
Fa la la la la la la la la.

See the groundhog rise before us
Fa la la la la la la la la.
As we sing the groundhog chorus
Fa la la la la la la la la.
Follow him as he ascends
Fa la la la la la la la la.
Join with true Great Groundhog friends
Fa la la la la la la la la.

Valentine's Day

★ CRAZY VALENTINE'S PARTY

Here are some great game ideas for Valentine's Day parties your kids will love.

1. *Valentine Bingo:* This is a mixer. Give each young person a sheet like the one on the next page. The object, like regular bingo, is to get five spaces in a row filled with signatures of people in the room who fit the descriptive phrases. To lengthen the game, after there is a winner, give the group ten minutes or so to see who can get the most names

VALENTINE BINGO

Has a Valentine's date	Saw "Love at First Bite"	Has had "MONO"	Is wearing Red	Had a crush on a teacher
Owns a heart-shaped locket	Is in love	Dated a taller girl or shorter guy	Likes the "Love Boat"	Forgot to give parents a Valentine's card
Has driven a "Love Bug"	Has more than one boyfriend	YOUR NAME	Has been given a hickey	Cries at romantic movies
Watches soap operas	Really had a flat tire on a date	Never been kissed	Hoping for a Special Valentine	Dated a boy named Todd, or Mark, or Lyndon, or Kevin, or oh well, Free Space!**
Dated a real loser last year	Is wearing red lipstick	Knows someone who has underwear with hearts on it	Will never get married	Kisses on the first date

*Fill in the names of boys the girls in your group date.

completed on their sheets. No one can sign his own name, except on free spaces.

2. *Spin the Bottle:* Here's a new version of this game. Put as many slips of paper as there are people into a large mayonnaise jar. After you have divided into two teams, sit in a circle. Spin the mayonnaise jar and wait for it to stop. The person it points to must draw a slip of paper and perform the required instructions. He earns points if he completes the instructions successfully. Here are some sample instructions.

For 25 points, get the group to guess "Three's Company" in less than two minutes, using *Charades* to communicate.

For between 1 and 25 points (sponsors judge), answer this question: "If you were marooned on a desert island, who would you want with you and why?"

For 40 points, finish the following poem: "Roses are red, violets are blue, I like a date who _____."

For 50 points, pick a member of the opposite sex and show us how you might propose marriage.

For 30 points, do a charade of your favorite movie actress in two minutes.

For 30 points, name three songs with the word "love" in the title.

3. *The Dating Game:* Ahead of time, choose four kids who you know can handle a role play. They take the role play cards and study them for a few minutes, while the rest of the group thinks up some questions to help the contestant. Set up a stage like the "Dating Game" television show, so the contestant cannot see the dates while asking questions and vice versa. On a blackboard list the questions to be asked the eligible dates. The contestant can use those or any others he thinks of. Introduce the contestant and the three eligible dates to the audience and play just like the "Dating Game." It's a riot.

Here are some sample role play instructions.

Dating Game Role Play

The Girls:

(1) Nancy

You are what one would call a Plain Jane. You are attractive but just never seem to get noticed. You are dying for a date; you would do anything for a date (almost). You overdo it and try too hard in all of your answers.

*You are from a small town in Nevada. Your hobbies include paint-by-number, helping sponsor a chess club, and emptying bed pans once a week at the nursing home.

(2) Candy

You are the typical dumb blonde. You are so naive you think Adam and Eve wore swimsuits. You are a knockout and get a lot of attention from guys, which you like, so you are a bit of a flirt and a bunch of a tease. You'd probably go out with anyone.

*You are from the Midwest, and your hobbies are tennis, swimming, and sun bathing. You were first runner-up in the annual Midwest Hog-calling and Cow-Chip Toss Contest.

(3) Zelda

You are a real heartthrob—good-looking, smart, great to be with. However, you know all of that, which makes you kind of a snob. You aren't too sure you want a date with our contestant. After all, he would have to be pretty good to get a chance with you.

*You are from New York, and your hobbies are fashion design, disco dancing, backgammon, and spitting at old ladies.

The Contestant:
Macho Max

Tall, handsome, and debonair, any girl would want a date with you. You are witty, charming, but not too egotistical. From a downhome family, you would make the ideal date. You are a really likeable, talented person.

*From Medusa, South Carolina, you like roller skating, underwater cooking, and jelly beans.

*Announcer's portion: Introduce the girls and contestant and ad lib.

4. *Valentine Charades:* Get a supply of those little candy conversation hearts with sayings, like Slick Chick, Kiss Me, and Be Mine. One person from the group picks one of the candies from a bowl, and using the regular rules for charades, tries to pantomime the message. The person who correctly guesses the saying eats that piece of candy.

 SWEAT HEARTS PARTY

Everyone has a sweethearts party or banquet on Valentine's Day; be creative and throw a Sweat Hearts Party. Ask everyone to come in athletic attire and plan an evening of wild games, races, and other sweaty events. It's fun and takes a lot of pressure off kids who are sometimes threatened by romantic Valentine's Day events.

 VALENTINE CAROLING

You've probably gone Christmas caroling, but have you gone Valentine caroling? Next Valentine's Day, have your group learn the songs below or any love songs that you know and serenade the people you love—parents, seniors, workers in the church, or neighbors. They will love it! If possible, dress everyone up in red and white and maybe one member of the group as Cupid. Present a box of candy, cookies, or a Valentine's Day card to the people.

(To the tune of "Jingle Bells")

Big red hearts
Flowered cards
Coming through the post
Valentines from someone who
You know will mean the most
(repeat)

Dashing through the snow
In a 4-door or a coupe
We have come to you
To knock you for a loop
Our songs we bring today
To take away your blue
Oh, what fun it is to sing
A Valentine to you

(To the tune of "Deck the Halls")

Deck the halls with hearts of gladness
Fa la la la la la la la la.
Tis the day we don't want sadness
Fa la la la la la la la la.
Don we now a big wide smile
Fa la la la la la la la la.
Sing we love in every mile
Fa la la la la la la la la.

(To the tune of "Mistletoe and Holly")

Here we are, it's dandy
It's time for Valentines and candy
Big red presents
Val-en-tine cards
Saying we love you so

Here we are and caring
It's time for loving
And for sharing
Kissing sweethearts
Big bright red cards
Spreading love wherever we go
(men) Happy Valentines . . .
(women) Happy Valentines . . .

(To the tune of "Oh, Christmas Tree")

Oh, Valentine
Oh, Valentine
We bring you love from Jesus
Oh, Valentine
Oh, Valentine
We bring you love from Jesus
His Love is true in summertime
But also in the wintertime
Oh, Valentine
Oh, Valentine
We bring you love from Jesus

(To the tune of "Jolly Old St. Nicholas)

Jolly old St. Valentine
How'd you ever know
That we'd need a special day
Today, "We love you so!"
Valentine's is here today
So we thought of you
We'll whisper how we love you so
That's just what we will do . . .

(To the tune of "We Wish You a Merry Christmas")

We wish you a happy Val'tines
We wish you a happy Val'tines

We wish you a happy Val'tines
And a happy heart day.
Good tidings to you
We'll love you always
Good tidings on Val'tines
And a happy heart day.

★ MYSTERY SWEETHEART BANQUET

If you have a youth group that is relatively free of serious romances and close to an equal number of boys and girls, here's a fun event for Valentine's Day. Plan a banquet or party where everyone has an instant date by drawing names out of a hat. If there are slightly more girls than guys or vice versa, use adult sponsors, borrow someone from another group, or put the appropriate number of girls' names in the boys' hat and vice versa. If someone has a date of the same sex, then it will really be a surprise. For couples who are going steady, encourage them "just this once" to join in the fun and develop some trust between them.

★ PARENT VALENTINE BANQUET

Sponsor a Valentine's Banquet for parents. The young people prepare and serve the meal to their parents, then do a program of skits and special music. Take lots of pictures, have lots of fun, and this may become an annual event.

Lincoln's/Washington's Birthday

★ PRESIDENT'S BIRTHDAY PARTY

If your young people get the day off to celebrate Abraham Lincoln's or George Washington's birthday, throw a big birthday party during the day and play lots of outdoor games. If you are celebrating Lincoln's birthday, divide into two teams: the Yanks and the Rebels. Then, wage Civil War, playing all kinds of competitive games. If you are celebrating Washington's birthday, then your teams can be the British (Redcoats) and the Colonists or perhaps the Yankees and the Doodles. Then, stage a Revolutionary War. Bake a giant birthday cake for refreshments and sing "Happy Birthday" to Abe or George.

St. Patrick's Day

★ **ST. PATRICK'S DAY SCAVENGER HUNT (p. 74).**

Easter

★ **EGGSTRAVAGANZA (p. 25)**

★ **GIANT EASTER EGG HUNT**
Kids build a giant Easter egg out of chicken wire and papier mâché about six feet high and hide it somewhere in the area. Plan a treasure hunt, described in chapter three, using the giant egg as the treasure.

Mother's Day/Father's Day

★ **MOTHER'S/FATHER'S DAY BANQUET**
Similar to the PARENT VALENTINE BANQUET (p. 165), schedule a Mother's/Father's Day Banquet on the day that falls exactly halfway between Mother's Day and Father's Day.

The Summer Months

★ BLIZZARD BLAST

Designed for a sweltering day in the middle of summer, "think snow" incorporates the use of ice or snow, even if it's make-believe. Teams can have names like The Snowdrifts or The Frosties. For refreshments, serve ice cream and snow cones, anything that is cold. Here are a few sample games to play.

1. *Snowball Fight:* Teams wad up stacks of newspaper into snowballs and throw them into the other team's territory. The team with the least amount of snow in their territory at the end of the game is the winner.

2. *Snowball Fight #2:* Fight with marshmallows; have everyone bring a bag.

3. *Ice-Melting Contest:* Each team gets a block of ice to melt, using only their hands (rubbing it). The ice is weighed at the beginning of the game and again at the end. The team whose block has lost the most weight wins.

4. *Ski Relay:* Make skis (old shoes nailed to strips of wood). The kids race in them. Snowshoes work well, too.

5. *Mining for Marbles:* Kids fish marbles out of a pan of crushed ice with their bare feet.

6. *Snowman Feed:* Hold a pie-eating contest, using lots of whipped cream. No hands are allowed.

★ BROAD SIDE OF A BARN

Try this on a warm, balmy summer night. Show a movie on the side of a building—barn, church, or storage building. Big buildings make great giant movie screens. Have the kids sit on blankets or bring lawn chairs. Serve popcorn and other refreshments.

CHRISTMAS IN JULY

This special event is really popular because it's so crazy. Organize a full-fledged Christmas party in the middle of summer. Decorate appropriately, sing Christmas carols, and have a gift exchange. Oftentimes, the Christmas story and the true meaning of Christmas makes a deeper impact at this time of the year when it is separated from all the hustle and bustle of the holidays.

OUT-OF-SCHOOL-FOR-THE-SUMMER PARTY

Most kids would enjoy a year-end party that celebrates no more school and the beginning of the summer. Here are some possible games.

1. *A Dunce Relay:* Divide into teams. One player on each team runs to the blackboard and writes "teacher is a dunce," then returns to his seat, and tags the next player on the team.

2. *Unspelling Bee:* Organized like a regular spelling bee, each word must be misspelled but still recognizable. Give an award for the most creative entry.

3. *Excuse List:* Each team tries to write the most excuses for not getting an assignment completed on time. Best list wins.

4. *Bubble-Gum-Blowing Contest:* When the teacher (adult) turns his back to the class, each student is given bubble gum and begins blowing bubbles. When the teacher turns around to face the class, the person with the biggest bubble seen by the teacher wins.

5. *Class-Notes Bonfire:* Have all the kids bring any class notes they don't want to save and send them up in flames. Do this in a fireplace or furnace, where it's safe.

PROGRESSIVE PICNIC

Adapt a regular progressive dinner for nice summer weather. Everyone should bring three or four paper plates, plastic forks, napkins, and cups. Each course is served outside on blankets or picnic tables. Go to several parks or use the backyards of the folks who prepare the food. Play a different outdoor game at each location to add to the fun. It's a nice change of pace.

★ PROGRESSIVE SPRINKLER PARTY

Several homes host the group, and everyone should wear bathing suits and bring towels. Set up sprinklers in the backyard of the first house, with a giant slip-n-slide to play on (make one out of huge sheets of plastic). Wage an organized water balloon war at the second house, with all the balloons prepared ahead of time. At the third house, play a volleyball game, with sprinklers going over the net. The last stop can be a house with a swimming pool.

Add any number of attractions along the way, especially if you live near a beach or near a giant water slide. Kids will love the variety of traditional and crazy water events.

★ SWIM PARTY

Summer is the perfect time for a beach or pool party. Next time you plan one, try some of these games.

1. *Across the Amazon:* String a rope across a swimming pool and have swimmers race across the pool pulling themselves hand-over-hand along the rope, perhaps relay-style.

2. *Aquatic Baseball:* This is a game of baseball in a swimming pool. Use a rubber ball about the size of a volleyball. The bases are marked on the four sides of the pool, like the diagram on the next page.

The team that is up provides its own pitcher, who tosses the ball to the batter, who hits the ball with his fist. The ball must stay in the pool to be a fair ball. After the ball is hit, the batter swims to the bases, as in regular baseball. The game can be simplified by having just one base plus home plate.

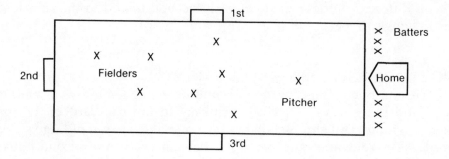

3. *Balloon Push:* Have swimmers race across the pool pushing balloons, wooden blocks, or anything else that floats with their noses.

4. *Boat Tug of War:* If you have canoes, kayaks, rafts, or rowboats, tie them together back-to-back for this game.

5. *Candle Races:* Swimmers try to carry a lighted candle around the goal and back swimming or walking in the water. It must stay lit the entire way.

6. *Crazy Canoe:* Two people get in a canoe or on a surfboard and with their hands, paddle in opposite directions. See who can get the farthest.

7. *Ding Ball:* String a net or rope across the pool or swimming area. Toss lots of balls out into the water. Two teams (one on each side) try to throw all the balls on the other side of the net. When the whistle blows, everyone stops throwing. The team with the least amount of balls on their side wins that round.

8. *In-and-Out Race:* Each team gets in a boat or raft and races to a goal. Every time the whistle is blown, everyone has to dive out of the boat and climb back in before continuing.

9. *Pearl Diving:* Use marbles or wrapped pieces of candy for pearls and toss a large amount into the pool. At the signal, the kids dive in and grab as many as they can. Assign point values to different colors, sizes, or kinds.

10. *Potato Race:* Kids race relay-style carrying a potato in a spoon.

11. *Somersault Race:* Swimmers race across the pool, but whenever a whistle is blown, they must do a somersault in the water before continuing.

12. *Sweatshirt Relay:* Team members race around a goal and back, relay-style, in the water with a sweatshirt on. When they tag the next player, the shirt must be transferred from one player to the next.

13. *Tube Races:* Kids race in inner tubes, paddling backward.

14. *Water Bronco:* Tie a long rope to a snow saucer or inner tube. Several kids pull a teammate across the pool on the saucer while he tries to stay on. It's a lot like water skiing.

15. *Ugly Dive Contest:* Kids compete to see who can do the worst-looking dive.

16. *Ice Push:* Teams push a twenty-five-pound ice block across the pool and back, relay-style.

 THIRTY-ONE WAYS TO COOL OFF

Here's a good idea for a summer ice cream party. Get a small amount of all thirty-one flavors of ice cream from a Baskin-Robbins Ice Cream Store and lots of sampler spoons. Provide a list of flavors from the store and number each container. Place them all on a table and allow the kids to sample each one trying to match the flavors with the ice cream. To add to the confusion, let the kids vote to determine which flavors are best, worst, or most unusual.

 WATER DAY

For this summertime event, you'll need a lawn, some hoses, a water tub, water balloons, and a few other odds and ends. Kids come in swimsuits or shorts, and games like those below are played. For refreshments, serve watermelon!

1. *Typhoon:* In this relay game, two teams line up facing a water source. At a signal, the first person in each line runs down to the water, fills a bucket, runs back to his team, and throws the water in the face of his teammate. Before throwing the water, his teammate must point and yell, "Typhoon!" Each person takes the bucket down to the water and returns to storm his team. The first team to finish is the winner.

2. *Bucket Brigade:* Teams line up single file, with a bucket full of water at one end of the line and an empty bucket on the other end. Each person in line has a paper cup. Team members try to transfer the water from the full bucket to the empty bucket by passing the water from one paper cup to the next. The team that transfers the most water within a time limit is the winner.

3. *Water Balloon War:* Make lots of water balloons and have a free-for-all.

4. *Volleyball in the Rain:* Play volleyball with a lawn sprinkler providing the rain. Other games can be played this way as well.

5. *Waddle-Walk Relay:* Contestants run a relay course with a water balloon held between their legs (they mustn't break it) and a cup of water on their heads (they mustn't spill it).

End of the Summer

★ **BACK-TO-SCHOOL NIGHT**

Best suited for the end of the summer, it can be given other names, such as End-of-the-Summer Blues Night or Back-to-School Boot Camp. Decorate the room in a schoolroom motif and tell the kids to arrive early enough not to be tardy. Each kid can bring a lunch pail or a sack lunch, with their name on it, to make it really seem like school. Before the event begins, the kids can gather in the schoolyard and play hopscotch, foursquare, and other playground games. Use a buzzer or school bell to start the activity.

In the Orientation, the principal explains what is going to happen. Then the students divide into classes (teams) for all the activities. Each class will get a grade (A,B,C,D, or F) for how they do in the games. At the end, figure the grade point average for each team to determine the winning class. Below are some ideas for the games, but feel free to substitute other games as well.

1. *Homeroom:* Play a variation of the BARNYARD game. Assign each team a sound to make. Next, have all the kids mingle, so all the teams are mixed up. When the lights go out, team members must close their eyes if it is not completely dark and make their sound until they find all the other members of their team. The first team to collect all their members is the winner.

2. *English Class:* Have the kids act out "What I Did During the Summer" as a Shakespearean play. The teachers (leaders) can judge for the most dramatic presentation.

3. *Speech Class:* Any game that involves speaking, such as the GOSSIP game—kids line up and the first person recites a phrase to the second person, and so on—can be played. Whichever team preserves the original phrase the best is the winner.

4. *Biology Class:* Have the teams dissect an avocado. Give each team a plastic knife, spoon, avocado, needle and thread, and instruct them to remove the pit and sew up the avocado. The best job wins.

5. *Gym Class:* Use any game that involves physical activity.

6. *Study Hall:* Play word games, such as Hangman (by teams) or Boggle.

7. *Between Classes:* No school day is complete without a trip or two to the locker. For this game, make a number of lockers out of hanging clothes bags. Inside each of the bags, put a stack of books, magazines, a can of soda pop, a tennis racquet, and a pair of gym shorts. Each member of a team must open the locker (unzip the bag), take out all of the contents and hold them while putting on the gym shorts. Then, he must close the locker, run to a specific point, and return back to the locker, and repeat everything in reverse order—open the locker, take off the shorts, replace the contents, close the locker, and run to tag a teammate, who must do the same thing.

8. *Lunch:* Play a game that involves food or serves refreshments.

The entire event can be conducted like a day at school with periods, breaks, recess, and going to the principal's office for discipline.

End of the Year

 ALL PURPOSE PARTY

There are several holidays that occur around the end of the year. With this All Purpose Party, celebrate them all at the same time and call it a Halloween-Thanksgiving-Christmas-New Year's Party and divide the evening into four segments of thirty or forty-five minutes of celebration for each holiday. Begin with a Halloween Party, complete with costumes, Halloween games, cider and doughnuts, and ghost stories. Next, move to another room decorated for Thanksgiving and serve turkey with all the trimmings. Then, move to a Christmas Party with a gift exchange, a visit from Santa, and Christmas carols. End the evening with a New Year's Party and have clocks appropriately set, so midnight comes when you want it. Provide noisemakers and sing a rousing chorus of "Auld Lang Syne." Schedule this four-in-one party in November or December.

Halloween

BOOB-TUBE BASH

Here's a good idea for a masquerade party. Have everyone come dressed as their favorite television character, past or present. After everyone has voted, announce the ratings (prizes) for the most original, the oldest television show, and best look-alike. Serve T.V. dinners or tube steaks (hot dogs) and play television games, such as "Name That Tune" and "Family Feud."

★ COSTUME SCAVENGER HUNT

Divide your group into scavenger hunt teams. Each team picks one member to be the person who gets costumed. Then the teams go door-to-door and get one item at each house that can be part of a costume for their team member. The team member puts on the item *as it is received*, so he adds to it as the group goes from house to house. One house might give them an old coat; another a wig; another some lipstick. At the end of the time limit, each team brings their Halloween model back to see who has the best costume. Award prizes for the funniest, most creative, scariest, and ugliest.

GROTESQUE SCAVENGER HUNT

Ideal for Halloween, this is a two-part scavenger hunt. Give each team a supply of zip-lock bags and a list of food items, like the ones below, which they must bring back within the time limit. Specify that only one item per house may be collected. No item from the garbage is allowed. But that's not the end of the scavenger hunt. When they return, they are given a bowl to mix all the items on the list after they have been checked in. Then, one or more members of the team must eat the whole mess and when finished, shout, "My compliments to the Chef!" The first team to do this is the winner.

1. ¼ cup of ketchup
2. 1 raw egg
3. 1 bone (any kind)
4. ¼ cup of mustard
5. ¼ cup of horseradish
6. ½ cup of flour
7. ½ cup of leftover vegetables (any kind)
8. Any portion of Jell-O or pudding
9. Two inches of toothpaste
10. Any portion of leftover meat (any kind)
11. A cup of coffee or tea
12. ½ cup of mayonnaise
13. ½ cup of refried beans

 GREAT PUMPKIN HUNT

Plan a treasure hunt (see chapter three) and hide the treasure—a giant pumpkin—somewhere in your area.

HALLOWEEN DINNER

This is a variation of the MYSTERY DINNER (p. 123). For your Halloween Dinner, disguise all the items on the menu with names like these:

1. Witches' Brew (punch)
2. Jack's Ripper (knife)
3. Devil's Right Arm (fork)
4. Grave Digger's Delight (spoon)
5. Bones (beans)
6. Slimy Shivers (Jell-O)
7. Dracula's Dream (meat)
8. Monster Mash (potatoes)

 PUMPKIN PARTY

Obtain a good supply of pumpkins or have the kids each bring a pumpkin with them for this crazy Halloween event. Listed below are just a few of the many possible games to play. For refreshments, serve pumpkin pie, pumpkin ice cream, and pumpkin cake and cookies!

1. *Pumpkin Carving:* See who can carve the craziest looking jack-o-lantern.

2. *Pumpkin Pitch:* Take the tops off some of the pumpkins (jack-o-lanterns) and pitch Ping-Pong balls into them for points.

3. *Pumpkin Bowling:* Set up milk-carton bowling pins and see how many kids can knock over with a small, round pumpkin.

4. *Pumpkin Push:* Contestants push a pumpkin around a goal and back, relay-style, using their heads.

5. *Pumpkin Caroling:* Lead the group in some of these inspiring songs or go Pumpkin Caroling around the neighborhood.

"Great Pumpkin Is Comin' To Town"

Oh, you better not shriek, you better not groan,
You better not howl, you better not moan.
Great Pumpkin is comin' to town!

He's going to find out from folks that he meets
Who deserves tricks and who deserves treats.
Great Pumpkin is comin' to town!

He'll search in every pumpkin patch,
Haunted houses far and near,
To see if you've been spreading gloom
Or bringing lots of cheer.

So, you better not shriek, you better not groan,
You better not howl, you better not moan,
Great Pumpkin is comin' to town!

"The Twelve Days of Halloween"

On the twelfth day of Halloween
My true love gave to me
Twelve bats a-flying,
Eleven masks a-leering,
Ten ghouls a-grooming,
Nine ghosts a-booing,
Eight monsters a-shrieking,
Seven pumpkins a-glowing,
Six goblins a-bobbling,
Five spooks a-scaring,
Four skeletons a-rattling,
Three black cats a-screeching,
Two trick-or-treaters a-running,
And an owl in a dead fir tree.

"I Heard the Bells on Halloween"

I heard the bells on Halloween
Their old, familiar carols scream.
And wild and sweet the words repeat
The pumpkin season's here again.

Then pealed the bells more loud and strong,
Great pumpkin comes before too long.
The good will get, the bad will fret,
The pumpkin season's here again.

"Pumpkin Wonderland"

Screech owls hoot, are you list'nin'?
'Neath the moon, all is glist'nin'—
A real scary sight, we're happy tonight,
Waitin' in a Pumpkin Wonderland.

In the patch we're waitin' for Great Pumpkin,
We've been waiting for this night all year,
For we've tried to be nice to everybody
And to grow a pumpkin patch that is sincere!

Later on, while we're eating
What we got trick-or-treating,
We'll share all our sacks of Halloween snacks,
Waiting in a Pumpkin Wonderland.

"I'm Dreaming of the Great Pumpkin"

I'm dreaming of the Great Pumpkin
Just like I do this time each year.
When he brings nice toys to good girls and boys
Who wait for him to appear.

I'm dreaming of the Great Pumpkin
With every pumpkin card I write.
May your jack-o-lanterns burn bright
When the Great Pumpkin visits you tonight.

"Pumpkin Bells"

Dashing through the streets
In our costumes bright and gay,
To each house we go
Laughing all the way.
Halloween is here,
Making spirits bright,
What fun it is to trick-or-treat
And sing pumpkin carols tonight!

Oh . . . Pumpkin Bells, Pumpkin Bells,
Ringing loud and clear.
Oh what fun Great Pumpkin brings
When Halloween is here!

6. *Pin the Nose on Jack:* Play just like Pin the Tail on the Donkey. Draw a large pumpkin on a piece of poster board and have the kids try to pin a nose in the proper spot while blindfolded.

SCARY SCAVENGER HUNT

Here's a scavenger hunt for Halloween. Some of the items, like the list below, are vague to allow the kids to be creative—find something that might fit the description.

1. A witch's eye (a marble)
2. A popcorn ball
3. A bat's wing (a chicken wing)
4. A voodoo doll complete with pins
5. Two feet of black streamers
6. A popped orange balloon
7. Any mask, the scariest wins
8. Four pieces of chicken corn candy
9. A dozen pumpkin seeds
10. Black cat fur
11. A bar of soap for somebody's window
12. A signature from someone, not in your group, who believes in ghosts

 SPOOKS SPREE

This is an old-fashioned Halloween carnival that your youth group can build. It features a variety of booths set up around the room (or outdoors) operated by the youth, with a different game in each one. Invite the church and the community. Promote the carnival as a free event or charge a certain amount per game and use the proceeds for your favorite project. Here are some sample games.

1. *The Cat's Meow:* Roll a Ping-Pong ball through an open cylinder (paper towel tube) to land in a flat pie tin.

2. *Apple Fish:* Tie a string with a weight onto a fishing pole and have the kids cast it through holes in the back of the booth. Apples should be tied on, and the string pulled back out.

3. *Ring Toss:* Chairs turned upside down provide four poles. Toss clothes hangers over them.

4. *Bean Bag:* Paint figures on the back of a booth with holes in the figures. Bean bags should be thrown through the holes.

5. *Plate Sailing:* Use four rinsed-out ice cream containers (large, can type) and have kids toss paper plates into them, Frisbee-style.

6. *Down the Hatch:* Drop clothespins into small bottles.

7. *Pumpkin Bowling:* Set up plastic containers and roll a small or medium-sized ball at them.

8. *Owling Inn:* Use small metal wastebaskets tilted against the wall at a 45-degree angle. Players get five Ping-Pong balls to bounce into them.

9. *Shot in the Dark:* Allow three squirts of a water pistol at a row of lighted candles. Only one candle needs to be extinguished.

10. *Ghost Hunt:* Hang white dishcloths on a cork surface and pin balloons in the center of the dishcloths. Use a black light, and the balloons will show up as dark spots on the white surface. Throw darts at the balloons.

11. *Ping-Pong Pumpkin:* Have kids toss Ping-Pong balls into pumpkins lighted inside by flashlights.

12. *Jack-O-Luck:* Cut a jack-o-lantern face out of a cardboard box and toss rubber balls through its holes. Light the inside of the box with flashlights.

13. *Peanut Pitch:* Throw peanuts onto a large outline of a peanut drawn on the floor. Peanuts that fall inside the outline win.

14. *Tic-Tac-Throw:* Throw bean bags onto a table with a large tic-tac-toe diagram on it.

15. *Pumpkin Looping:* Use coat hangers made into a circle or plastic hoops to toss around pumpkins.

16. *Squirt Box:* Kids are given squirt guns, water balloons, or pies to throw at their favorite youth sponsor or parent.

WITCH HUNT

In this treasure hunt (see chapter three), the treasure is a witch. Either a real person dressed up like a witch or life-sized witch doll can be brought back by the winning team.

Thanksgiving

 THANKSGIVING SCAVENGER HUNT

Give kids a list of food items and have them try to find as many of them as possible within the time limit. After the food has been collected, it can be donated to needy families or to an organization that distributes food to the poor.

 TURKEY EVE GOBBLE-ATION

Here's an event that's good for Turkey Eve (the Wednesday night before Thanksgiving), although it can be planned anytime around Thanksgiving with a different name.

Kids bring food to be donated to needy families and deliver it, if possible, before the activities begin. Then, everyone meets back at the church or at someone's home for an evening of fun. Games can include the following:

1. *Turkey Shoot:* Draw two large turkeys on paper that can be covered with a sheet of glass. Use toy suction-cup dart guns, which shoot about twenty feet. The turkeys are divided into eight sections, with each section naming a particular action to be performed. There are two teams, and each team has a gun. Each team elects a Team Turkey, who stands in front of the entire group. Team A shoots at their turkey, and whatever action they hit, Team B's turkey must do, and vice versa. The crazier the actions, the better—Gobble Like a Turkey, Flap Your Wings, or Hop Around Your Team on One Foot.

2. *Turkey-Gobbling Contest:* Get several volunteers to participate in a Gobbling Contest to see who can gobble the loudest. However, all but one of the contestants is clued in ahead of time and knows that the joke is on one particular volunteer. When the leader counts to three, everyone is to gobble as loudly as he can, but the only one who gobbles is the one person who is unaware that the others have been told not to gobble.

3. *Turkey-Decorating Contest:* Give teams a stack of newspaper, construction paper, tape, and other similar items and have them decorate one of their team members as a turkey. The best-dressed turkey wins.

4. *Turkey of the Year:* Prior to the event, have people vote for Turkey of the Year with money. Post pictures of the nominees somewhere in the church where everyone can see them. Voters put money in a jar (with a slot in the lid) for their favorite Turkey of the Year. Each nominee campaigns with a sample gobble in church or a campaign speech for another turkey nominee. At the party, reveal the winner and crown him Turkey of the Year complete with all the trimmings (throne and crown).

Christmas

★ CAROLING TREASURE HUNT

Here's a great way to go Christmas caroling this year. Divide into caroling groups for a treasure hunt (see chapter three). Each group is given a first clue to find the location of the first place where they are to sing Christmas carols. It could be at someone's home, at a rest home, or at a shopping center. The group must go there and sing all verses of at least four Christmas carols (chosen ahead of time), ending with "We Wish You a Merry Christmas." They either pick up the next clue or have the next clue already with them in a sealed envelope and go to the next location, and so on. Schedule the caroling groups so none of them duplicate locations. If locations need to be used more than once, make sure each group has a different set of songs. The last destination is the location of a Christmas party with refreshments and games.

★ CHRISTMAS SHOPPING SPREE

Many times kids cannot buy Christmas gifts for the family without little brother or sister watching (we all know what squealers little brother and sister are). So, this Christmas, plan a Christmas Shopping Spree for your youth group. Take the group to a big shopping mall or some other place where there are lots of shops with a good selection of inexpensive gifts. Let them take an hour or two to shop together. Kids enjoy shopping with their friends, especially junior highers. After an afternoon or evening of shopping, return to the church or someone's home for refreshments and a Gift-wrapping Party.

★ **CHRISTMAS COSTUME PARTY**

Ask everyone to come dressed as a character or thing that is associated with Christmas or the Christmas story. Ideas for costumes can come from the Bible or from any other Christmas tradition—Santa, Frosty the Snowman, or Scrooge.

CRAZY CAROLING CONTEST

Crazy Caroling is creative Christmas caroling. Divide into caroling teams and give each group a set of instructions, like the list below. Everybody starts from the same place and returns at the end of the specified time or when they have completed all ten items.

Instructions:

1. Go to houses in the neighborhood and at each house sing a carol while following one of the directions below.
2. After you have completed the carol, get the signature of a resident of the house in the space provided.
3. Do a different number at each house, only one per house.
4. Thirty-minute time limit. Do all you can in that time.
5. Have fun and spread some Christmas cheer!

Caroling Directions:

1. Sing all verses of a carol (in the book) backward.
2. Sing a carol over the phone to Charlie (889–0781).
3. Sing a carol sitting cross-legged (Indian-style) on the porch.
4. Sing a carol opera-style.
5. Form a human pyramid and sing a carol.
6. Sing a carol to someone under five years of age.
7. Sing a carol in a kitchen.
8. Sing a carol around a Christmas tree.
9. Sing a carol to someone over sixty years of age.
10. Sing all three verses of "Deck the Hall" and *act out* all the lines, with everyone participating, and ham it up.

SANTA CLAUS HOSTAGE PARTY

Santa Claus, who has been kidnapped by terrorists, is the treasure to be found. Give teams a copy of a ransom note explaining that Santa has been kidnapped and that unless certain demands are met, Santa will be exterminated. The note can also include a clue that begins the hunt. The first team to bring him back gets a reward. Use the other treasure hunt suggestions in chapter three to design your own event. End the hunt with a party, caroling, and any other holiday ideas you have.

★ CHAPTER NINE ★

Fun Fund Raisers

Here are some great socials and special events that will double nicely as fund raisers. They are fun to do and serve a very useful purpose. Money raised can be used to help finance the youth ministry of the church or to support a mission or service project of the group's choosing. For more great fund-raising ideas, see *Ideas For Social Action* (by Anthony Campolo, Zondervan/Youth Specialties, 1983).

★ BIBLICAL ICE-CREAM FESTIVAL

Set up an ice cream parlor with a biblical theme. Choose a good location, advertise it well, and invite people to try some Heavenly Ice Cream Delights created by your group. If possible, get the ice cream donated or purchased at wholesale prices.

Decide on prices for each item—high enough that you will be able to make some money, but not too high. Serve free coffee or punch with each order. Members of the youth group can prepare the ice cream dishes, wait on tables, and clean up. Suggest they dress in biblical garb, just for atmosphere.

See the sample menu on the next page.

★ CARHOP FRY-OUT

Have the kids turn the church parking lot into an old-fashioned drive-in restaurant, with carhops on roller skates, greasy hamburgers,

Menu

The Sea of Galilee
A two-scoop vanilla island whose shores are washed by a blue-tinted 7-UP ocean.

The Sunday Sundae
One scoop of strawberry ice cream surrounded by six teaspoon-sized scoops of vanilla ice cream.

Pontius Pie
Take command of the situation by ordering a slice of Pontius Pie—an ice cream and graham cracker spectacular, distinctly Roman.

The Red Sea Split
A vanilla ice cream trough filled with homemade strawberry topping for those who desire freedom from the slavery of hunger.

Samson and Delilah
A sensuous scoop of vanilla covered with a seductive topping, sharing the dish with a Samson-sized scoop of chocolate ice cream covered with a full head of chocolate-chip hair.

Joseph's Cone of Many Colors
A cone of rainbow sherbet to refresh you on your way to Egypt (or anywhere else).

The Garden of Eaten
A well-coordinated blend of fruity ice cream and toppings, complete with a snake to tempt you to have another.

Shadrach, Meshach, and Abednego
Three princely kinds of ice cream surrounded by a fiery furnace of Red Hots.

John the Baptist
A unique blend of ice cream, honey, and locust-shaped almonds to create a most magnificent creation.

Tower of Babel
A towering combination of assorted ice creams covered with a variety of toppings, whipped cream, and nuts.

Palm Sundae
Two scoops of vanilla ice cream covered with coconuts and enhanced with a decorative palm frond.

and the whole works. Invite the community to come and eat in their cars while the kids serve hamburgers, hot dogs, milk shakes, and French fries. Set up a P.A. system that will play oldies but goodies to add to the atmosphere. Charge enough to make a profit for your project.

 DINNER THEATER

Here's a fund raiser that everyone enjoys. Pick a weekend, find a good location (the church's fellowship hall), and put on a Dinner Theater, featuring good food and a theatrical performance by the youth group. Plan it to be serious, with a well-rehearsed play and gourmet cooking or more tongue-in-cheek, with goofy looking waiters, mediocre food, and some crazy skits and fun entertainment.

The key to the success of your Dinner Theater will be adequate preparation and enthusiasm on the part of the youth group. Everybody can get involved, either with the food, the decorations, the publicity, or the entertainment. Tickets can be sold for several weeks in advance to insure a sell-out crowd for both Friday and Saturday night. One youth group raised over $4,000 in a single weekend, and everybody had a great time.

DRIVE-IN MOVIE NIGHT

If your church has a big parking lot or a large, useable area, set up a large movie screen at one end of the parking lot and a 16mm projector and a few large speakers (you might be able to hang the screen over the side of the building). If you are in a heavily populated neighborhood, you may need to check the local ordinances, or with the neighbors, about the potential noise that might be generated.

Invite all of your church and neighborhood to come to the Drive-in Movie Night. You can charge admission per car or per person or provide it free of charge. Have the kids make popcorn and set up a refreshment stand with drinks and other goodies.

★ GRANOLA PARTY

Have the youth group get together for a Granola Party to make their own special brand of granola that can be sold later. Find a good recipe—preferably one that includes lots of "good stuff" like nuts, banana chips, carob chips, coconut, grains, honey, and other nutritious ingredients. Have the kids prepare the granola in large quantities, bag it in sealable plastic bags, and put it in decorated coffee cans. It can be sold door-to-door or to friends and relatives.

★ LE GRAND CHÂTEAU

This fund raiser is great fun for everyone. Open "for one night only" your own fine French restaurant—an elegant dining experience that includes classy entertainment. However, the catch is the small print at the bottom of the menu: "Management reserves the right to make substitutions without patron consent." So, regardless of what people order, they all get the same thing.

The menu should look like a regular menu (with the exception of the catch line at the bottom) befitting a fancy French restaurant, featuring elaborate and extravagant dishes at high prices. The publicity should include a snooty "reservations only," so the right amount of food can be prepared.

The dress code should be ties for the gentlemen and dresses for the ladies. Decorations should be elegant—cut flowers, candles, linen on the tables, and classical music. The waiters should be dressed to the hilt, with the *maitre d'* in tux if possible. The food should be nice but simple—juice, tossed salad, baked chicken, baked potato, vegetable, roll, dessert.

After dinner, allow a few minutes to explain your project and how the proceeds of the evening will be used, then a program of your choice. At the close, the waiters can present the cheque to each customer, instructing people to make their donations in any amount and to pay

Le Grand Château

Entrées

Includes dinner roll, dessert, and hot beverage

Storione à la Cardinale	*Bigginaccá de Renaldois*
$11.55	*$8.90*
New York Steak	*Fischer Fried Chicken*
$9.20	*$8.75*
Veal Marengo and Gamberi	*Arthur's Perogy Geschmäck*
$13.60	*$9.00*
Dumpling Dewar Stew	*Lobster Waikiki*
$5.00	*$8.65*

(children's portions available upon request)

Appetizers $4.00 ea.

Escargot   Galettes au Fromage   Canapes
Frogs Legs   Bongo Bongo

Floor Shows commence at 7:30 & 9:30 P.M.

Management reserves the right to substitution without patron consent

either their waiter or on their way out. Usually, a special event like this is very successful and worth all the work involved.

PARENTS NIGHT-OUT

This is a good way for the youth group to do something nice for their parents and other adults in the church, as well as make a little money for the group.

Offer the parents and adults a Night-Out that gives them dinner, a movie, and baby-sitting—all for one low price. Rent a 16mm movie or a video and show it on a giant screen.

Have the group prepare and set up for the dinner, then divide them in half. One half serves the adults; the other half feeds and cares for the children in another room. Then they switch. Half the group does cleanup; the other half baby-sits. Afterward, all the youth work together to put everything away and see the movie, if there's time.

 SAMPLE FAIR

This idea takes a few months to prepare, but it is very effective as a fund raiser because it is different enough to attract a lot of attention. First, write a form letter, like the one on the following page, to various companies that provide products, foods, or services. Send it to nationally known companies or to local companies and perhaps contact some of these personally with a phone call or visit. Ask them to give you a large quantity of free samples for your Sample Fair.

If a letter like this is sent to enough companies, you can get hundreds of different free samples for your Sample Fair. Tickets to the Sample Fair can be sold for whatever price you feel is reasonable, and your kids can pass out the samples at the fair, one to a customer. Some companies may provide plastic bags for people to collect things, or they may send a representative to help explain the product. At any rate, the overhead is low and the benefits are high. You can also provide a refreshment booth and sell baked goods and concessions to add to the festivities of a fun evening that raises a lot of money for a worthwhile cause.

Dear Sirs:

Would you like us to promote your product?

Our senior-high youth group has decided to raise money to purchase a _____ for our church. We are calling our project a Sample Fair. To be successful, we are asking you to help . . . and in return, we will be helping you promote your product.

Here is our request: Do you have a sample or pass-out item for promotion? This will not be sold. Tickets in advance and at the door will be sold to entitle each person to one of each sample. To complete the evening, the youth will present a Home Talent Show.

We're certain the samples will create interest and excitement, so we will have good attendance. If you are interested and care to help us with your samples, we would be very pleased. Our goal is to sell three hundred tickets. Our Sample Fair will be on _____ in our church fellowship room.

Thank you very much.

Sincerely,

★ SOUP SUPPER

Prepare lots of soup and have a soup extravaganza that people pay to attend. Either enlist the help of members in the congregation who know how to cook up a pot of delicious homemade soup or create your own special concoctions by combining cans of commercially prepared soup, adding other ingredients to make the soup unique. Serve salad, bread, and a beverage and provide small cups so the people can sample lots of different soups. Charge enough at the door to turn a little profit for your project. Advertise it well, and there will be a good response.

★ SUPERSUB SALE

A couple of weeks before Super Bowl Sunday, put a flyer in your church bulletin announcing that your youth group is sponsoring a Supersub Sale (submarine sandwiches) on Super Bowl Sunday for whatever cause the youth group is supporting. Make the ad very appealing and include the price of the sub, when to pick them up (deliver them to make it even more desirable), a possible list of ingredients, and a tear-off order coupon with name, address, phone number.

Plan a Supersub-making Party the Saturday night before Super Bowl Sunday to make all the sandwiches that have been ordered and enough sandwiches to feed the group as well. Wrap and refrigerate the subs to insure freshness.

★ WORLD HUNGER BANQUET

This event will raise money for world hunger and also raise the consciousness of the group regarding world hunger. Plan a banquet and program and invite everyone to attend. The food should be served buffet-style—the following entrees on a table with signs indicating the price of each item. Explain to everyone that they can order their choice of food, but they may NOT EXCEED thirteen cents, which represents the daily food budget of most of the world's population. They pick up their food and pay the cashier at the end of the table.

Menu

Water — 1¢
Coffee — 6¢ a cup
Sugar — 2¢
Milk — 2¢
Saltines — 1¢ each
American cheese — 6¢
Radishes — 1¢ a serving

Olives — 2¢ each
Orange slices — 8¢ each
Hard-boiled eggs — 6¢ each
Carrots — 3¢ a serving
Sweet pickles — 2¢ a serving
Raisins — 9¢ a serving
Cookies — 3¢ each

Following the meal itself, lead a discussion concerning the problem of world hunger and ask everyone to become personally involved. To begin, suggest that people give the difference between what they paid for their meal (thirteen cents) and what they might have paid for a regular meal at a restaurant. Some people will want to give more. Then, send the money to an agency working to fight world hunger.

★ CHAPTER TEN ★

And More!

This chapter contains more outstanding special event ideas and socials that didn't quite fit in the other nine chapters. So rather than leave them out, we've included them here.

★ ALL-NIGHT EVENTS

If you ever have difficulty getting your group together for an evening event because of schedule conflicts, try this. Plan an all-night event, such as bowling or skating, that doesn't begin until around 11 P.M. Kids love it and are usually available. Include plenty of physical activity (to keep everyone awake) and lots of food and refreshments. End with breakfast.

★ BEDROOM BLITZ

Here's a fun activity that helps your group get better acquainted. Have the group meet at the church (or any other location) and then travel together to visit the bedrooms of each member of the group. Make sure everyone has plenty of advance warning to prepare his bedroom. Each bedroom occupant gives a guided tour of his bedroom by telling about the things that are hanging on the walls or from the ceiling. The group can also meet each person's parents and other family members. At the last house, have a party and give awards to the messiest room, the most unbelievable room, the biggest room, the loudest room, the best-decorated room, and the neatest room.

★ BOARD-GAME ROTATION

Next time you do a Board-Game Night, try this. Set up tables in a circle with a different two-player board game on each table. Put chairs on two sides of the table with half of the chairs facing out and half the chairs facing in, comprising an inner-team circle and an outer-team circle.

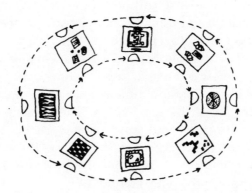

Have everyone take a seat. The games begin and continue until the whistle is blown after about five minutes. Both of the circles then rotate to their right, so each person now moves to a different game with a different opponent and begins playing where the last player stopped. For example, a person might move from a winning checkers game to a losing position in Yahtzee. Each game is worth a set amount and each team given credit for the win, then the games begin again.

★ BUS DRIVE-IN

Take your youth group to a drive-in movie in a bus. Park in the back, parallel to the screen, and have the kids sit on top of the bus or in lawn chairs beside the bus to watch the show. Arrange the sound boxes so that everyone can hear. Talk with the theater management ahead of time and arrange for some discount prices. Be certain the movie is suitable for all ages.

 ## CARD PARTY

Here's a good idea to use the next time you would like to honor somebody in a special way on his birthday, anniversary, graduation, or some other occasion. Get together for a Card Party and divide into groups to make the special-occasion cards. Give each group some construction paper, a few old magazines, a pair of scissors and glue, and marking pens. Each group's assignment is to make a card, using word cutouts and photos from the magazines. The message can be strung together ransom-note-style and say whatever the group chooses. Nothing can be written on the card except for the signatures of the people in the group who made it. After the cards are finished, mail or deliver them to the appropriate recipients.

 ## DESTINATION UNKNOWN

Have kids meet in the morning for a day of activities that remain a secret to everyone in the group, except the youth sponsors. Include a picnic, an outdoor game, a trip to an amusement park, dinner in a restaurant, a party afterward, or whatever your time and budget will allow. Kids enjoy the mystery of it.

FAMILY FILM NIGHT

Sponsor a film night for families in your church and neighborhood on a regular basis. Borrow good films from the public library (Disney films, old time comedies) and show them on a big screen. Your youth group can provide popcorn and other refreshments or ask people to bring snacks to share.

★ GROUP BIRTHDAY PARTY

If your kids enjoy celebrations, one you would not want to overlook is the birthday of your youth group. After you have made a good guess when your church's very first youth meeting was held (you may have to pick a day if you don't know), celebrate it with a party every year. Order a cake from the local bakery. Decorate with streamers and balloons and give everyone party hats and favors.

Play a variety of games, and if possible, try to coordinate them with your youth group. For example, create a Youth Group Trivia Game, using names and information from the last year or from the distant past. Of course, no birthday party would be complete without opening gifts. Perhaps the youth sponsors could share pleasant memories or slides of each youth from the past year as a gift; the youth may wish to share their favorite memories as well. Maybe the youth sponsors could present to the group a gift, which they have made or purchased (athletic equipment, a picture for the wall, a game) to be used by the group for years to come. Make this an annual event.

★ HANG-OUT PARTY

Sometimes kids just need a place to "hang out," so have a Hang-out Party. Pick a place where kids will feel comfortable, provide some music, a television set, some video games, card or board games, refreshments (very important), and some very inconspicuous chaperons. Encourage kids to come and just "hang out"—bring a friend, a favorite game to play, or even homework.

HOME MOVIE NIGHT

Ask the kids in your group to bring some of their families' favorite home movies or video movies to show to the entire group. If you have lots of film, get several projectors or television sets and show several films at once, around the room. By having more than one movie playing, the odds of having long, boring segments are reduced, and you create an arts-film-festival atmosphere. As a variation, have each person show and narrate, if necessary, one short home movie segment. Serve popcorn and other movie-type refreshments.

 INDOOR HAYRIDE

Here's how to have a hayride when you have lousy weather. Fill a bus with hay, enough to put about two feet of hay all over the floor and the seats. Better yet, find a bus that has all the seats removed but make sure there are windows for ventilation, since the dust gets quite thick at times. It's a great way to go Christmas caroling.

★ **INSTANT REPLAY**

Here's a good After-the-Football-Game Event or a Fifth-Quarter Event. Pick the biggest game of the season and videotape it and the halftime activities. See if you can put one camera in the press box at the stadium and another on the sidelines for some close-up shots. At your party, show these video highlights on a giant-screen television. For best results, make sure you have good video equipment and people who know how to operate them.

If advertised well, you will attract a lot of kids and automatically gain an audience with the football teams, the bands, the drill team, and the cheerleaders. Invite new kids to come to your youth group. Serve refreshments and create a warm, comfortable atmosphere.

★ KIDNAP EVENTS

If you think you can successfully hide something from your youth group, try this activity. Plan a special event but don't tell the kids about it, only their parents. The parents find some way to keep their kids home on the day or night of the event when the kids are kidnapped by the youth sponsors and taken to a surprise location for the activity. It could be a 5 A.M. Kidnap Breakfast or a Kidnap All-Night Film Festival. Complete surprise is essential.

★ LOCK-OUT

Many youth groups have had great success with a Lock-in, when kids spend the night together *inside* a church building playing games, watching films, and camping on the floor. Just to be different, try a Lock-out, when the kids stay *outside* the church in the parking lot, on the lawn, or in some other place. Plan all the things you would normally do at a Lock-in, with the additions of stargazing, outdoor cooking, and perhaps a sunrise service.

 PARTY FOR OTHERS
Here's how to turn your next social or special event into a service project. Throw a party, not for yourselves, but for someone else. Plan a Sweethearts Banquet for an old-folks home or for the elderly of your church; an Easter Egg Hunt for an orphanage or special education group; a Christmas Party for underprivileged kids; or a Thanksgiving Banquet for widows, college students, or servicemen. The possibilities are endless. It's a great way to do something nice for others and have a lot of fun at the same time.

 PORTA PARTY
Please and surprise even your older youth by coming at an unexpected time (during a regularly scheduled meeting) carrying a suitcase filled with a Porta Party. For any outrageous reason, such as random birthdays or National Pickle Week or for no reason at all, stage an instant party by bounding into the room with your party hat and your suitcase filled with a cake, ice cream, bowls, spoons, napkins, and streamers. Be creative, have a Porta Party at some kid's house 6 A.M. on the morning of his birthday. Your Porta Party will be talked about and remembered for a long time.

 RAIN DANCE
So often, our most carefully made plans for an outdoor event are laid to rest by rain or foul weather. Just for the fun of it, put a date on

your calendar to be canceled in the event of sunshine! Call it a Rain Dance or a Rain-out and plan activities to do in the rain, like volleyball, water balloon wars, and mud fights.

VIDEO PARTY

Stage a Video Party for kids to make their own Music Videos. The kids lip-sync some of their favorite records, air-band-style, or dramatize the song as they sing it. No real instruments are allowed, for example, they may use a tennis racquet for a guitar and trash cans for drums. You will need one or two video cameras and someone who knows how to operate them properly. Divide into groups, and film each one separately and in a separate room. Then, watch the finished videos together afterward for a lot of fun.

★ Y'NO

Y'no how everybody says, "Y'no?" Next time you have a party or special event, y'no, call it Y'No, which stands for Youth Night-Out. It's a pretty simple idea, y'no, but the group will love it.

★ WORLD'S LARGEST PILLOW FIGHT

For this crazy event, you'll need a room large enough (and durable enough) to accommodate a lot of action. Have each person bring a pillow from home. Begin your event with a few regular games or other preliminaries before you have the actual pillow fight. If you include music or entertainment, kids can sit on their pillows.

Schedule the pillow fight as the last item on the program and organize it well. Kids are not allowed to hit anyone with their pillows until they are given the signal. Outline the boundaries for the pillow fight on the floor. When everyone is ready, begin the fight. Run the fight in one-minute periods with a bell or whistle to stop the action. Anyone who hits somebody after the bell is out or if a person's pillow breaks, he is automatically out. Make sure kids use soft pillows and don't put anything inside the pillow cases except the pillows. Use common sense, take safety precautions, and this event can be a feathery as well as fun activity.